SECRETS OF LATERAL THINKING

101 IDEAS FOR THINKING CREATIVELY

"Everyone is a genius at least once a year. The real geniuses simply have their bright ideas closer together."

Georg Christoph Lichtenberg, physicist (1742–99)

SECRETS OF LATERAL THINKING

101 IDEAS FOR THINKING CREATIVELY

ROB EASTAWAY

SHELTER HARBOR PRESS
NEW YORK

SECRETS OF LATERAL THINKING

Rob Eastaway

This book was originally published in 2007 under the title: *Out of the Box, 100 Ideas for Thinking Creatively*

This 2016 edition printed for Shelter Harbor Press by arrangement with EMEX LTD

Shelter Harbor Press
603 West 115th Street, Suite 163
New York, NY 10025

For sales, please contact:
info@shelterharborpress.com

Managing Editor: Caroline Ball
Editor: Katie John
Editorial Assistant: Kirty Topiwala
Managing Designer: Clare Thorpe
Designer: Mala Hassett
Commissioned illustrations: Bonnie Dain for Lilla Rogers Studio

ISBN: 978-978-1-62795-050-3

10 9 8 7 6 5 4 3 2 1

Typeset in Trade Gothic
Colour reproduction by Scanhouse, Malaysia
Printed and bound in China by Imago

CONTENTS

Introduction   8

CHAPTER 1 RECOGNIZING CREATIVITY   12
Box? What box?   14
Finding your creative streak   20

CHAPTER 2 A CREATIVE ATTITUDE   24
Getting out of the rut   26
Identifying personal blocks   29
Getting positive feedback   31
Avoiding premature evaluation   35
Turning whines into problems   36
Beyond the expert view   38
The "What if?" game   40
Right time, right place   42
Building confidence   44
Just do it!   47

CHAPTER 3 THINKING AROUND A PROBLEM   50
Answering a different question   52
A child's-eye view   54
Simple questions   56
Starting at the end   59
Listening to your daydreams   60

Comparing and contrasting   62
Reversing a problem   65
Lateral thinking exercises   68

INTERLUDE: THE MESSINESS OF CREATIVITY   70

CHAPTER 4 GENERATING IDEAS   74
Where do ideas come from?   76
Warming up your mind   78
Patterns of thought   80
Doing something totally different   82
Seeking a second opinion   83
Inspirational people   84
Bending reality   86
Figuratively speaking   90
Old idea + old idea = new idea   92
Storing ideas   95
Serendipity   96
When words collide   98
Picking a theme   101
Having a Plan B   103

CHAPTER 5 BEING CREATIVE WITH OTHERS   104
Holding discussions   106
Swapping ideas   108
Working in large groups   112
Brainstorming   114
When differences get personal   116
Suggest, don't propose   119
Finding three positives   121
Looking for a third way   124
Seeing the funny side   126

CHAPTER 6 MAKING IT HAPPEN   128
Setting a deadline   130
Beating the mid-project blues   132
Planning for the worst case   134
Ten words for creativity   135

Solutions   136
Index   139
Further reading   144
Acknowledgments   144

INTRODUCTION

You've picked up this book because you want to expand your horizons. Perhaps you'd like to start a new career or learn a new creative skill. Perhaps you'd like to get out of your usual routine and make your daily life more fulfilling. Here, you'll discover original styles of thinking that can enrich every part of your life. Whatever your goals, the ideas and techniques in this book can help you unleash your imagination, overcome challenges and realize even your most ambitious dreams.

JOINING THE DOTS

To test your thinking skills, you might start by going back to the Victorian puzzle that first inspired the popular phrase, "thinking outside the box". In case you haven't seen the puzzle, here it is. Draw nine dots in a square, like this:

Your challenge now is to join all nine dots, using straight lines only, and without your pen or pencil leaving the paper. Can you put at least one line through each of the dots using only four strokes?

You'll quickly find a way of joining all the dots with five lines – for example, like this:

If this puzzle is new to you and you manage to come up with the four-line solution, then you're exceptional. (For the classic four-line solution, see page 136.)

Why do so few people succeed in finding the four-line answer? They get caught out because, when first trying to solve the puzzle, most people (including me when I first saw it) regard the square shape as a boundary and keep all the lines inside it.

It's quite a shock to think that we all tend to get trapped in this way, but we do so for a reason. To think outside the box seems inefficient, a waste of time or to some people even irrational. And yet it turns out that finding an approach which, in the short term, seems "irrational" proves to be the only way to come up with a perfectly rational solution.

However clichéd this puzzle may have become, I still think it's one of the best illustrations of the challenge of thinking creatively. We make assumptions all the time, creating our own artificial boxes, and it doesn't occur to us that we might need to go outside them. It turns out, however, that for the most logical of reasons, to think out of the box we sometimes have to allow ourselves periods of irrational "play".

CAN YOU LEARN TO BE CREATIVE?

As you embark on the challenge of thinking more creatively, you might notice a little voice of doubt whispering in your ear. Can you really do this? Maybe you simply aren't a creative thinker. Isn't creativity a gift that only the chosen few are born with?

Let me debunk this great creativity myth straight away. Labelling people as either "creative" or "uncreative" can be as unhelpful as labelling people "athletic" or "unathletic". In an age where tens of thousands of ordinary folk take part in city marathons, everyone recognizes that athletic ability lies on a spectrum, and that with practice it's possible for everyone, whatever their ability, to improve. Creative thinking is no different – you really can learn to think out of the box. There's no magic here, because we aren't talking about inventing a new skill, but more about recapturing a skill that life has squashed out of you.

RE-IGNITING YOUR CREATIVE SPARK

All of us are born creative. As children we experiment and challenge everything: "Why do I have to go to school?" "Why can't I stay up until midnight?" "Why can't I go to the moon?"

Society, school and eventually work do a lot to stifle our creativity. We're taught to find logically right answers, but not the imaginative yet wrong answers that go beyond the bounds of "normality". Most of us have had the experience of coming up with an idea, only to have other people telling us things like, "No, that would never work," or "We've already tried that." On top of that, given the hectic lifestyles that most of us have in the modern world, many people simply feel they don't have the time to step back and be creative, even if they want to. I hope this book will convince you that it's worth finding space in your daily schedule to pursue your dreams and ideas. I hope it will also help to provide you with the confidence and know-how to give free rein to your talents.

The tips and techniques in this book should help you whatever your ambitions. However, I should point out – because creative thinking books often don't – that not every technique applies to every situation. To take an extreme example, if you're trying to think of a name for a newsletter, then brainstorming with a group of people will probably help. But if you're planning on writing a novel, then you'll be better off using more solitary methods of inspiration. (As far as I know, Charles Dickens didn't sit around with colleagues, unfold a flipchart and announce, "OK, let's have some ideas for Chapter One.")

Whatever your creative challenge, big or small, I hope that reading this book will inspire you to try something new.

"When I let go of what I am, I become what I might be."

Lao Tzu (6th century BC)

CHAPTER 1

RECOGNIZING CREATIVITY

Box? What box? 14

Finding your creative streak 20

To make the best use of your creativity, it's vital both to identify your skills and to be aware of any habits that might be holding you back. Before you can think "out of the box", you have to figure out what your "box" is.

This chapter begins with a few light-hearted exercises. These games are intended to be fun, but they also show you new possibilities and alert you to assumptions that may be limiting your ideas. Later on, you're encouraged to think about your creative skills, including any that you've not yet recognized. The chapter ends with some guidance on how to use your creativity in the best way for you.

BOX? WHAT BOX?

Before you can break out of the box, it helps to remind yourself what it feels like to be in it. Here are a few exercises that illustrate various kinds of "inside the box" thinking. If you find yourself trapped by any of these habits, you're in good company – most people have the same problems.

THE SWIMMING POOL PUZZLE

The Robinson family had a square swimming pool in their garden. At the corners of the pool were four trees. The Robinsons wanted their pool to be twice as big, and still square. However, they weren't allowed to cut down the trees. How did they solve the problem?

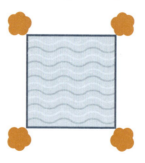

Children usually offer creative solutions to this problem, such as:

- Put the trees on islands and dig around them.
- Make the pool twice as deep.
- Build a double-decker swimming pool with a slide.

All of these are great ideas, though there's a simple solution that most children and adults miss (see page 136). Sometimes you just need to look at a problem from a different direction.

EASY AS ABC?

You might be surprised how much the ideas you have are influenced by patterns you grew up with. Try the following exercise.

If   **ABC** ⟶ **ABD**   then **XYZ** ⟶ ?

Think of an answer now, before you read ahead.

If your answer was XYA, you thought the same as the vast majority of adults. When a clock gets to 12.00, it goes back to 1 again. Many people apply the same pattern to letters: after "Z", they go back to "A". There's nothing wrong with this answer, but it's not the only one.

Here are some others that people have come up with: XY1; XY, then blank space; XYD; WYZ; XYAA. Some of these answers might strike you as creative, particularly the answer XYAA. How did this person come up with the idea of adding another letter?

As it happens, the woman who gave me the answer XYAA thought it was "obvious". She used a spreadsheet every day, and the column after Z in a spreadsheet is AA. When I put forward the answer XYA, she said, "Oh, I like that — who thought of that one?" You may not have thought of her idea, but nor would she have thought of yours. New ideas sometimes depend simply on having a different experience.

101 USES FOR A DRIED-UP PEN

You need to have a pencil, paper and a clock or egg-timer for this exercise. Once you're ready, imagine that you've just been presented with a cheap ballpoint pen, made out of clear plastic. The pen has one big drawback: it's run out of ink. Give yourself one minute to write down as many things as you can think of that you can do with the inkless pen.

Start … now.

- Most people find this exercise difficult, and come up with no more than three ideas. The most common idea of all is: "throw the pen away and forget about it."
- Some people think of four or five ideas. Typically, they'll think of practical ways in which they've already used a defunct ballpoint pen – for example, as a pointer, or for punching a hole.
- A few people score much higher. I've known the odd individual score as high as 15.

You can see some of the different uses to which people have put the inkless pen on page 136, and this is just the start. Given time, between us we could probably find as many as a thousand ideas.

Whatever the challenge, there's always a huge pool of ideas to draw from, and once you recognize this fact you'll have taken an important step toward freeing your creativity. Later in the book you'll find plenty of ways to tap into that ideas pool.

NOT JUST A SILLY ANSWER

On certain TV quiz shows, contestants are given multiple-choice questions. Sometimes, to make the selection easier, there's an answer that's clearly right, one or two that are wrong with a moment's thought, and one that's stupid. The answer is often so obvious that it's an insult to the intelligence — but sometimes the silliest answer can be the right one. For example, look at the following question:

What was the name of the first self-service supermarket in the USA?

- Safeway
- Safe-buy
- Piggly Wiggly?

In fact, Piggly Wiggly, founded in 1916, was the first supermarket, and is familiar throughout the Southern and Midwestern USA. The founder said he chose the name precisely because it sounded so silly. Once you'd heard the words "Piggly Wiggly", you were never going to forget them — or his supermarket.

CRAZY NAMES

There are many ideas that at first sight seem silly, but in hindsight make sense because they're so memorable. The companies choosing the product names Amazon (what's that got to do with books?), Lexus (snappy word, but doesn't immediately suggest "car") and Apple (an edible computer?) might have had second thoughts about them. Yet today the names are so established that the public might be affronted if they were ever changed.

A SURPRISE IN THE MIRROR

How often have you looked in a mirror in your lifetime? Probably thousands of times. With all that experience you ought to have no problem with the following question.

Imagine you're standing close to a vertical mirror (such as a door on a bathroom cabinet), and can see down to your navel. You step back a few feet. Can you now see: (a) more of yourself (b) the same amount (c) less of yourself?

Most people "know" that the answer is (a) — but they're wrong. The answer is, in fact, (b): as you step back from the mirror, you

can still only see down to your navel. I wouldn't be surprised if you don't believe me, and rush off to find the nearest mirror to test this out.

Why do people get this wrong? Probably because mirrors are often tilted downward slightly, so when you step back from them you do see more of yourself. When you're confronted by a new problem, it's natural to look for similarities to situations that you've encountered before. But although the problem you're facing now might look the same as certain aspects of your past experience, perhaps it's subtly different in some way. Your existing knowledge can sometimes mislead you.

THE "AHA!" MOMENT

One theme that connects all of the exercises so far is that they all contained surprises. At the start, you probably looked at a particular situation one way, and by the end you may have found yourself looking at the situation quite differently.

Much of creativity is about enjoying this experience of surprise, which some people call the "Aha!" moment. Other experiences that often result from creative activities are the sense of pride in creating something beautiful, and perhaps also exhilaration and even laughter.

The philosopher Arthur Koestler once described creativity as being about three things: art, discovery and humour. Somebody else found a neat way of encapsulating this:

Creativity is about **AH!**, **AHA!** and **HA HA!**

If you felt frustrated that the "Aha!" moments didn't come to you until you'd sneaked a look in the back of the book, don't worry – you're not alone. Few people can summon up "Aha!" moments at will, but with practice and the right attitude, they do begin to happen more often. In the words of the great innovator Thomas Edison: "Creativity is 99 percent perspiration and one percent inspiration." And those moments of inspiration are so satisfying that it's well worth the wait.

"Be an opener of doors."

Ralph Waldo Emerson (1803–82)

FINDING YOUR CREATIVE STREAK

Creativity doesn't just exist among world-famous artists and Nobel prizewinners. Think about your relatives and friends: what are their talents? Some may have special skills, while others may simply use their gifts as part of daily life. In the same way, you may find the seeds of creativity in yourself.

WHAT ARE "CREATIVE THINKERS" LIKE?

Creativity comes in many forms. To find your own definition, think of a few people you know whom you'd describe as creative. For each one, identify their talents and attitudes. Almost certainly they have quite different attributes from each other. Here are the first few on my list:

Tom – a builder

When you ask Tom to take on a project, he always offers lots of ideas. And he'll quickly find a neat and elegant way around any problem.

Laurie – a PR executive

She looks at the world a different way from most people and finds angles that are unconventional, but (usually) work. She also has a dry, quick sense of humour, which can be great for sparking new ideas.

Richard – a composer

As well as composing music, he's a great enthusiast about life. Tell him about a new idea, and he'll invariably see the possibilities.

Kelly – a cook (in her spare time)

Give her a brief and she'll create what you want but with clever extras. She's a perfectionist, driven to keep refining her ideas right to the end.

ELEMENTS OF CREATIVITY

Each person in the list above has a combination of skill and outlook that makes him or her good at what they do. By looking at them, we can identify traits that go with creativity.

A creative thinker might be someone who:

- Generates plenty of ideas.
- Can instinctively tell which ideas work and which don't.
- Approaches things at a different angle from everyone else.
- Challenges everything.
- Builds on your ideas rather than knocking them.
- Is driven by a desire to create things.
- Is never stopped by a problem for long.
- Sees connections between apparently unrelated worlds.
- Fine-tunes ideas until they work perfectly.

You need to bear in mind that it's unusual for anyone to have all these attributes in all situations. If Tom and Laurie swapped jobs, their creative side might not show at all.

Now think about yourself. What are your creative attributes? Where are your weaknesses? Recognizing when you use skill, imagination and flexibility should highlight your own creativity. And by identifying any weak areas, you'll know what you need to work on.

HOW DO YOU WANT TO BE CREATIVE?

In a week, month or year's time, how will you know that you've become more creative? Decide what you mean by being creative, and measure yourself on that.

Perhaps you'll judge yourself simply on whether or not you produce something. The act of making a pot, or assembling a piece of furniture, may be the key that releases you from your "box", even if getting there felt more like a slog than a series of inspirations.

To some people, being creative means doing something different. That might mean something unlike anything you've done in the past, or creating something that nobody has come up with before, such as a unique painting or a new piece of music.

The second of these challenges is much harder, particularly if you don't just want to create something unique but also want to be happy with the result. After all, anyone can create a new work of art, simply by tipping some jars of paint onto a canvas. But is it art? Is it any good? That depends on you and the viewers.

Or finally, your main concern could be how you feel about yourself. Is your goal to feel engaged and fulfilled by what you're doing, without worrying too much about any end-products?

If the sort of creativity that excites you is experiment and discovery for their own sake, then you're in good company. Leonardo da Vinci was renowned for being great at coming up with ideas but hopeless at finishing projects. His main creative pleasure seems to have come from exploring new concepts, as his sketchbooks crammed with sketches for everything from bicycles to war machines make clear.

THE THREE PS

People generally judge whether an activity is creative by using three criteria, which I call the three Ps of creativity:

- The **Product** ("this painting is really different").
- The **Process** ("she got around so many barriers along the way").
- The **Person** ("it's creative because John Lennon wrote it").

If you ask people for an example of something creative that they've done, most will struggle. That's because they're trying to think of Products, and most people's jobs don't give them the chance to create things that are different.

The assumed link between the Person and creativity can become a self-fulfilling prophecy. People who are labelled "creative" will have creativity read into everything they do (think of Picasso, da Vinci, Mozart). "Uncreative" people might have similar ideas, but their talents may go unrecognized.

For many people, the most important part of creativity is the Process, or how you solve problems on the way to creating something. If you decide to make a chair, you'll need to do plenty of creative thinking about how it should look, how to find the materials, and how you'll put the pieces together. It might end up looking like a thousand other chairs, and you might not change others' perception of your creativity, but you might break out of many "boxes" to make it.

The Process aspect is perhaps the most useful for our purposes. It's important to recognize that most day-to-day creativity is about the journey and not the destination.

CHAPTER 2

A CREATIVE ATTITUDE

Getting out of the rut 26

Identifying personal blocks 29

Getting positive feedback 31

Avoiding premature evaluation 35

Turning whines into problems 36

Beyond the expert view 38

The "What if?" game 40

Right time, right place 42

Building confidence 44

Just do it! 47

Creative thinking is about having ideas, but just as importantly, it's an attitude. The most important elements are optimism and an open-minded approach. Just as optimists will see a glass as half-full rather than half-empty, creative thinkers will approach projects and challenges with a positive attitude. They'll focus on what can be done, and won't let problems or doubts bring their work to a halt. Creative people will also take leaps into the unknown, rather than sticking within their own comfort zone.

So how much of a creative thinker are you now? And what can you do to change your attitude, to help you think more creatively? This chapter looks at some of the blocks to accepting new ideas, and offers ways to help you adapt your approach to different situations.

GETTING OUT OF THE RUT

Are you in a rut? Do you feel you're just repeating the same routines day after day, or feel bored, frustrated and unsatisfied? In the days of horse-drawn carts, it took a big sideways jolt to get a cart out of a rut in the road. You may need to do something equally drastic to break out of your rut.

TRAPPED ... OR ARE YOU?

If you've found yourself in a rut, you need to identify what's keeping you there. You'll need different tactics depending on the problem. Most probably, you want to get out, except that either:

- You feel trapped (financially, physically, or because you have obligations that you can't get out of).
- You're comfortable (the rut is familiar, causes you no grief, and is a place where you feel confident – I've heard this situation described as a "fur-lined rut").

To escape from a rut that's trapping you, you need to think like Indiana Jones. Are you really trapped? Or is there a weak link somewhere, the equivalent of that loose stone, narrow ledge or chink of light in the ceiling, where you can begin to plot your escape?

Can you really not afford to look for another job? Do you really have to prepare your children's packed lunches at the same time every morning before facing the stress of driving the children to school? Somewhere, something might give if you put a little pressure on it.

To escape from a comfortable rut is just as hard, because even if you're unhappy with where you are, there are lots of little perks that keep tempting you to stay put. Given a choice between this security and the great unknown, it's not surprising that many people find themselves "stuck" in highly lucrative jobs that they hate.

BREAKING OUT OF YOUR COMFORT ZONE

The diagram below helps to illustrate what's happening. Where you want to be might be better than where you are now – but you may first have to go through an unsettling period in which things feel worse. If you're not prepared for the discomfort that comes with change, then every time you dip a toe in the water you'll quickly step out again. (Anyone who has tried to give up smoking will recognize this graph.)

Level of comfort

To get out of this trap, you either need enough motivation to help you put up with some pain on the way, or you need to find a way of leaping straight to your goal, bypassing the uncomfortable middle zone.

Making a snap decision

One way to make the big leap is by a sudden and irrevocable decision – perhaps resigning from your job or selling your house. If your feelings are strong enough, they may propel you through the uncomfortable stage. We all feel this desire for radical change at some time, but you need to seize the moment. Unless you put your plans into action straight away, it can be too easy to change your mind and backtrack after a good night's sleep. Once you've embarked on your new course of action, you also need to have regular goals to aim for, to keep up your momentum and prevent second thoughts from creeping in.

Tempting fate

Another escape route can appear if fate gives you a push: let's say, your company goes bust, or you face a family crisis that forces you to change your lifestyle. The snag is that fate is, by definition, out of your control. On the other hand, perhaps you can influence the course of your life a little. Start taking more risks, gambling with your future by taking on assignments where you aren't so sure of the outcome, pushing your limits. Something might just snap – and you might end up being very grateful that it did.

"To win without risk is to triumph without glory."

Pierre Corneille, playwright (1606–84)

IDENTIFYING PERSONAL BLOCKS

Some of the possible blocks to creative thinking may come from your environment – both your physical surroundings and the people in your life. However, it's more likely the main blocks you face will be personal barriers, such as low self-confidence and the way you organize your time.

COMMON PROBLEMS

The list below includes some of the most common reasons why people feel unable to use their talents. Do any of them strike a chord with you? What other issues might be holding you back?

"I don't have ideas"

This is the most common creative block. Often, people dismiss their own ideas as unoriginal or impractical. Or, if you're in a job dominated by rules and procedures, where mistakes aren't tolerated, you may feel you simply aren't allowed to have ideas. It's true that some people are more fluent at producing ideas than others, but it's impossible to think and not have ideas. Don't judge yourself against the creative geniuses: start from the way you are now.

"What will other people think?"

We can all feel anxious when we step out of the crowd, worrying that others might think we're rocking the boat, going beyond our abilities or perhaps going crazy. But, frankly, other people's opinions are their problem, not yours. By all means sound out trusted friends on your ideas – but you're doing this for yourself, not for other people. Creativity can sometimes be a lonely path, but it's a path that millions have trodden before you.

"I don't have the time"

Is this a block, or is it just an excuse? If it's really important, you'll make the time. Later in this chapter there are some suggestions for finding extra time. In any case, a lack of time isn't always a bad thing – sometimes, it can actually help you to have ideas. Working to a tight deadline, you don't have time to think too hard about the drawbacks. That's one reason why improvised comedy is often funnier than scripted comedy that has been worked on for months.

"What if it goes wrong?"

There are two reasons to be concerned about things going wrong. The first is that the mistake may be costly for you or others. If this is likely to be so, then of course you need to think through the consequences of your idea. But you shouldn't stop having the idea in the first place. The second concern is that your reputation will be damaged. (I still recall my one effort at karaoke singing – it'll take a lot to persuade me to try that again!) Again, don't let this deter you: one trait that marks out many great thinkers is their ability to keep on trying, even if they suffer embarrassing failures along the way. I like the attitude of the inventor Buckminster Fuller, who said: "There is no such thing as a failed experiment, only experiments with unexpected outcomes."

GETTING POSITIVE FEEDBACK

When you're trying something for the first time, you might look for feedback from your surroundings, other people or even yourself to help you judge how you're doing. Negative feedback can put you off, perhaps even permanently, but positive feedback can be vital to reinforce your efforts.

SPOTTING VICIOUS CIRCLES

When I was taking piano lessons as a child, I used to dread the sound of my own stumbling efforts to thump out a tune. Every wrong note would resound around the room as a reminder of just how badly I was playing. And of course every mistake undermined my confidence, and made it even more likely that the next note would be a mistake, too.

This sort of negative feedback can make creating or achieving anything extremely difficult. Each mistake reinforces the problem, as in the "vicious circle" below:

Make a mistake

ANXIETY: THE VICIOUS CIRCLE

Feel tentative about your next step

Become more anxious about being hopeless

BREAKING THE PATTERN

How do you break out of this negative loop? I discovered one way when I took up the piano again as an adult. I wanted to try pieces of music that I knew were far harder than I was able to play, so I invested in an electronic keyboard. Its most helpful feature was that it had a volume dial. To start with, I turned the volume down. It's amazing how much better your playing seems when you can hardly hear the duff notes!

This effect was enhanced if I put on a CD of the music I was trying to play, and turned the volume dial down close to zero on the keyboard. Now all I could hear was what it would sound like if I were playing perfectly, and I was getting a sense of what my fingers would feel like when doing it. I'm convinced that having this experience at the start motivated me to do the hard practice that followed.

When you want to try a new project or skill, it can help to spend some time deliberately exposing yourself to positive feedback and "turning down" the negative, at least at the start.

TURNING DOWN NEGATIVE FEEDBACK

There are various techniques that you can adopt to help you "turn down" negative feedback. Two examples are given below.

If you want to break out of your box by singing

The negative feedback is often the look on other people's faces or the sound of your own voice. To tune it out, sing in the car. Put on your favourite album (to drown yourself out!), get out on the road and open your lungs. At 60mph, nobody, not even you, can hear you scream.

If you want to break out of your box by drawing

One way to practise drawing is to copy a picture or a photograph. Unfortunately, many people find that when they compare their work to the image that they're working from, they can immediately see that the drawing "looks wrong".

The reason why your picture of, say, a face might look wrong is often that you don't copy exactly what you see. Instead, your brain overrides what your eyes have registered, and reproduces a standard image of a face that it has already generated from the faces you've seen in the past. As a result, you get confused when you try to draw what's in front of you.

One of the best ways to correct this confusing feedback is to turn the image that you're copying upside down. Your brain will no longer recognize the lines as a face (or whatever the image is), so you can concentrate on what you see, not what you think you see. The results can be remarkably accurate.

MAKING MAJOR CHANGES

The need to turn down negative feedback can be just as important in life's more serious challenges – both temporary changes, such as losing weight, and more long-term ones, such as changing your job.

If you want to break out of your box by dieting

Many people who go on a diet suffer negative feedback from standing on the scales and seeing that they haven't lost enough weight, and from their inner voice berating them for their lack of willpower. This makes them depressed, so they reach for a comforting snack – and so the vicious circle continues. If you face these problems, try hiding the scales and sticking encouraging messages to yourself on your kitchen cupboards and refrigerator, as a double whammy to break the loop.

If you want to break out of your box by changing your job

If you're planning a big change, such as shifting to a lower-paid but more fulfilling job, the negative feedback might come from friends saying, "Are you sure?" and your bank balance saying, "Look, I'm getting smaller!". Both of these factors may tempt you to stay in the "fur-lined rut" described on page 26.

This feedback is important (I find that ignoring my bank balance usually leads to a shock), but you need to control it. Ask your friends to give you the good points about your plans before saying what's wrong. And plan your finances in detail, so that even if your income drops, you'll be able to deal with the consequences. (You can find more advice in "Planning for the worst case" on page 134.)

AVOIDING PREMATURE EVALUATION

Next time somebody asks for your opinion about a new idea, notice your immediate reaction. Do you find yourself saying something like, "You couldn't do that because …", or "Ah, what you don't know is …"? Responses like these are natural, but they can kill the creative process stone dead.

THE SHOCK OF THE NEW

Why do we tend to react so negatively? In some cases, we have the best of intentions: we don't want the person to waste their time and energy. However, we might also do it for the following reasons:

- **We're brought up to look for correct answers.** Faced with an idea that isn't perfect, we feel obliged to point out its flaws.
- **New ideas can be threatening.** Their existence may make us feel that we're not doing our job properly, or that we need to change.
- **There's also a bias against ideas that are "not invented here".** Ideas often seem so much better when they're "ours".

Dennis Sherwood, a guru in the world of innovation, calls this negative reaction "premature evaluation", and reckons that it's a particular problem with young, dominant males!

Evaluation is important, but premature evaluation doesn't just snuff out someone else's creative spark: it also stops us from seeing new possibilities. Learn to pause whenever you hear a new idea, and take time to think about it and look for the good points.

TURNING WHINES INTO PROBLEMS

Even the most positive person likes to have the occasional outburst of complaining: "Why can't I ever find a parking space?" "Why do we have to have so many commercials on television?" "Why is this house always so filthy?" However, if you want a situation to change for the better, you need to do something, not just talk about the issue.

WHAT'S THE DIFFERENCE?

First, you need to be able to tell the difference between a complaint and a problem. Complaints are typically grumbles about things over which you have no control. They might feel therapeutic, but don't kid yourself that they'll improve your situation. Indeed, there are times when people indulge in complaining – or whining, as I prefer to call it – as a way of blaming somebody else, when they have no intention of putting the situation right themselves.

A problem, on the other hand, is a situation that you can influence and want to change. However big or complicated it is, you should be able to find something you can do to make a difference.

CHANGING YOUR APPROACH

One important step to improving your creativity is to "re-frame", or change your view of, the challenges in your life. You need to turn these issues from unproductive complaints or whining into problems that you can really get your teeth into.

Next time you face a difficulty, examine your own response as truthfully as you can. Watch out for statements that you could summarize as "It's not fair!" or "It's their fault!" Blaming other people, or life in general, won't get you anywhere. Instead, think of problems as starting with the question, "How …?" The table below illustrates some examples.

WHINE	PROBLEM
"Why can't they fix that noisy photocopier?"	"How can I find out who's responsible for the photocopier?"
"The traffic's always backed up at this intersection!"	"How can I find another way to get to my destination?"
"The snacks we get here are lousy!"	"How can I persuade the caterers to improve the snacks we get here?" (or "How can I bring in my own snacks tomorrow?")
"My wife/husband/partner doesn't understand me."	"How can I see it from his/her point of view?" or "How can I change my actions to get him/her to respond differently?"

The crucial part here is that you're taking responsibility for your situation. You're turning your response from "Why don't they do something about it?" to "What can I do about it?" This exercise also helps you to dig deeper into your real motivations. Is your moan really about a problem that you want to solve, or is it simply serving as an excuse for not doing anything, and therefore letting you off the hook?

BEYOND THE EXPERT VIEW

The world needs experts. Where would we be without scientists who can interpret DNA, or lawyers who can get their heads around tax fraud? However, seeing yourself as an expert can stop you thinking out of the box. A fresh outlook is much more likely to help you find new ideas.

BE LESS LIKE AN "EXPERT" …

I have a slightly cynical definition of an expert: somebody who knows every reason why a new idea won't work. It was experts who made the following disastrous pronouncements.

"Who the hell wants to hear actors talk?"

H.M. Warner, 1927

"Guitar groups are on their way out."

Decca Recording Co. turning down the Beatles, 1962

Do you ever go into "expert mode" when you're talking about wine, gardening or something else that you're particularly knowledgeable about? How do you demonstrate your knowledge to other people?

Much of the time, you probably do it by responding to their ideas with comments like "That wouldn't work because …" or "They tried that back in 1986 …" While it may boost your ego to demonstrate expertise like this, it's also a surefire way of killing off ideas.

... AND MORE LIKE A CHILD

Adults are often overly concerned about thinking and saying what they're expected to think rather than what they really think. Young children have a refreshing honesty about them, and divert their energy to new things that excite them.

I've heard it said that there are three stages of life:

From **0 to 4 years** old is the **"Why not?"** stage.
From **5 to 11 years** old is the **"Why?"** stage.
From **12 onward** is the **"Because"** stage.

The education system and the pressures of teenage life combine to make us into rational, conforming individuals who look for right answers rather than interesting ones. We become "Because" people – similar to the "expert" I described above.

To be more creative, you need to recapture some of the behaviour of your childhood. However, you need to be child-like, as opposed to childish. So I don't mean you should throw tantrums, make people buy you ice cream or laugh when someone falls over. What I mean by "child-like" behaviour is the curiosity and wonder about the world that leads us to ask those crucial questions, "Why?" and "Why Not?"

"For every expert there is an equal and opposite expert."

Anonymous

THE "WHAT IF?" GAME

Next to "Why not?", the most creative pair of words in the English language is probably "What if?" These two words open up your imagination and lead you to explore new worlds. You can begin to exercise your imagination by playing "What if?" games, by yourself or with friends.

WHAT A CRAZY IDEA!

To play a "What if?" game, you need to start with something that couldn't or wouldn't happen in the world as we know it. As an example: "What if I had a clockwork TV and I had to wind it up before I could use it?" What a mad suggestion! But that's the point. New ideas often seem ridiculous until we've thought them through.

So a clockwork TV would be a pain, that's for sure – you'd have to keep getting up to wind it, and it could run out of power at a crucial moment in a movie. And it might be quite tiring to keep on winding.

On the other hand … you'd certainly be more selective about what you watched. How about powering the TV with an exercise bike? Lots of people pay to go to gyms, but you'd be getting fit for free. You'd spend less time as a couch potato. So would your children – wouldn't this be the answer for the "TV generation"?

The idea of a clockwork TV might have its impractical side, but with all those benefits, it can hardly be dismissed as crazy. In fact, we already have the clockwork radio, one of the most successful innovations in recent years, which took Africa by storm in the 1990s.

HOW TO PLAY

You can come up with your own "What if?" examples, and make them as eccentric or fantastical as you like. Here are some more "What ifs" that you could try. Your challenge is to think of at least three potential good consequences, however outrageous the suggestion.

* * * * *

What if you could eat computers?

* * *

What if you had to train as an entertainer before you were allowed to have children?

* * *

What if plastic bags cost as much as a movie ticket?

* * *

What if your salary was paid into your bank account in small amounts every hour instead of a lump sum every month?

* * *

What if restaurants paid you to eat there?

* * *

What if the sky were green?

"A man with a new idea is a crank until the idea succeeds."

Mark Twain (1835–1910)

RIGHT TIME, RIGHT PLACE

If you want to increase your skills and stretch your imagination, you need the right setting as well as the right topic. In addition, it helps to set aside time. However, bear in mind that ideas don't always fit into a timetable. When the creative mood strikes, be ready to run with it.

LOOKING FOR SUPPORT

How is it that during the weekend your brain can be buzzing with ideas and projects and excitement, yet when it comes to Monday morning, everything feels as if it's been switched off?

This enormous swing in mental energy is down to three factors:

- **The people around you** – your attitude may reflect whether they're interested in you and receptive to your ideas or whether they undermine your confidence.
- **The place** – a bar full of people may make you feel buzzy, an art gallery reflective, while the boss's office might be intimidating.
- **The subject** – if it's something you're fascinated by or know plenty about, you'll have lots of ideas and opinions, but if you feel ignorant or uninspired, then the opposite will apply.

Try to surround yourself with people who give you the confidence to express your ideas. Choose a place that makes you feel inspired. And if the subject doesn't fill you with enthusiasm, look for ways to make it more exciting (see Chapter 4).

SETTING ASIDE A TIME

If you want to work on a creative skill or project, you need to make a plan and stick to it. Set a date and an amount of time a week or two ahead. Have in mind a task you'd like to accomplish – the more you focus on a specific activity, the more important that event becomes in your mind. The following steps should help you keep to your plan:

Be realistic about how much time you allocate

If you set aside a whole day, you might get cold feet about taking such a large chunk out of your routine. But if you allocate only 10 minutes, you have no reason to duck out. If you feel you can't take even 10 minutes out of your schedule, you might need to examine the way you organize your life, or look at your motivation.

Avoid distractions

You might find that other people's demands make inroads into your appointed creative time. To reduce the risk of being side-tracked like this, you could plan to do your creative activity somewhere you don't expect to be interrupted. Mark the booking on your calendar, in thick red pen, so that it's visibly important to you and everyone else.

Commit yourself financially

Perhaps the best way of committing to time out is by paying for it. It's easy to cancel something that's free, but if you've paid even a small sum for a ticket, a room booking or a professional person, then cancelling feels that much harder.

BUILDING CONFIDENCE

When you're facing a new challenge, especially if it involves skills and talents you haven't used before, it's essential that you boost your confidence. There's no need to let nervousness, or fear that you're not good enough, slow you down or even make you give up before you start.

STARTING SMALL

Whatever your ultimate ambition, the best way to tackle it might be to begin with a small or simple task. Often, the sheer scale of a task can make it seem all but impossible. If this is true for you, try to break the challenge down into small steps.

Alternatively, start with a goal that you feel you should easily be able to achieve – one that doesn't need too much time, planning or inspiration. For example, if you want to get into creative writing, trying to embark on your first novel is probably not a good idea, unless you're sure you have the resilience to be in it for the long haul; writing a diary is a much easier starting point.

At this stage, don't worry about how original your ideas are. Just by taking on a small challenge and succeeding, you'll prove to yourself that you can achieve objectives if you set your mind to them.

TAKING THE FIRST STEPS

There are plenty of small creative challenges you could set yourself, depending on the skills or ideas that you want to develop.

The list below gives some common ones, and shows how you can make them easier by progressing step by step.

Writing your autobiography

Start by producing a photo album of one episode in your life: a vacation, a year, a special event. The prospect of sorting through a whole life's stories and pictures could be so intimidating that you might never even start. However, by selecting just one period, you give yourself a much more manageable task.

Becoming a creative chef

Start with a quick but unusual meal that you saw being prepared on a TV show. Choose a meal that you can make from regular ingredients.

Refurbishing an old house

Start with a small room in which a relatively modest amount of work makes a large difference to the room's appearance. (Painting beats plumbing in this regard.)

Getting involved in community projects or local politics

Begin by writing a letter to your local newspaper or community website about an issue that interests or concerns you. Keep it simple — sometimes the shortest letters are the ones with the most impact.

Any of these simple techniques can help you to break out of your "box", giving you the confidence to go on to greater things.

FAKING IT

It's easy to do down your creativity. You usually know where your own ideas have come from, so they may not feel much like "Aha!" moments. It's wonderful when ideas arise spontaneously, but they can equally well come from artificial sources.

People who believe creativity is supposed to come from their own talent can find it difficult to accept that they can use techniques to help them. I was once working with a group of people who claimed to be hopeless at drawing. I showed them the standard technique for drawing faces (see page 33), which is simply to copy an upside-down picture or photograph. Almost everyone was impressed by the result, except for one person, who said, "But this isn't drawing." He assumed that, because he was using a trick, his drawing wasn't valid.

Professional artists also use "tricks", from copying photographs to using computer software. At first, using artificial aids to help you generate ideas may not seem creative at all, but the more you do it, the more natural it becomes and the more imaginative you can be.

CAMERA OBSCURA

Artists have been "faking it" for centuries. One drawing aid reputedly used by Leonardo da Vinci, Vermeer and Canaletto was the camera obscura. This device is a darkened box or room with a tiny opening at one end to let in light. The light will cast an inverted image of whatever is on the other side of the opening. You can use a mirror to reflect the image the right way up, then trace the outlines. However, even if these artists did use the camera obscura, it didn't detract from their overall skill.

JUST DO IT!

Nothing can be more intimidating than a blank sheet of paper. Whether your challenge is thinking of somewhere to go on vacation or something more ambitious, the opening few minutes … or hours … can be painful. Authors famously call it "writer's block". So how do you start?

IT DOESN'T HAVE TO BE PERFECT

Many artists, writers and composers will tell you the same thing. Just start somewhere. Anywhere. And don't be concerned about producing anything good in the first instance. The mere act of jotting down "any old rubbish" on a piece of paper can be enough to get the juices working. This is a one-person brainstorm, where you dump all your ideas without attempting to judge them on their quality.

Sometimes the only way to create something good is by producing something bad first. I once had a job on a team with a boss who was notoriously poor at briefing us when we wrote reports for him. We'd spend hours writing what we thought he wanted, only for him to cover our work with red ink and turn it into his own version. At first, we felt we were wasting our time, but then it dawned on us that our work acted as the catalyst for our boss's thinking.

The same principle can apply to your own work. An hour spent scribbling out a first draft that you finally throw away is not a waste of time. The mere act of getting these ideas down on paper lets you start to develop your thinking.

GETTING STARTED

Here are some more tips on getting started. They can all help to buy you some time, while you wait for your first inspiration.

* * * * *

Begin with an easy part.

* * *

Start at the end – the final chapter, the card you attach to the gift, the "thank you" speech when you've received your award for excellence.

* * *

Don't worry about the "creative" parts, but start on the chores: filing the cuttings, buying the tools or collecting the reference books.

* * *

Prepare a place to do your creative thinking.

* * *

Make a mark – any mark, even a doodle – on the page. It's a small gesture to prove that you've advanced beyond the blank sheet of paper.

* * *

Call a friend to tell them about how you're starting, why you're finding it hard and what you're planning to do about it. (Even if you don't know, you may find the very act of phoning somebody kick-starts the process.)

"Ready, Fire, Aim!"

Executive at chocolate manufacturer Cadbury

TAKING A CHANCE

If you're entering a competition or taking some other risk where the odds are stacked against you, it's all too easy to look at the chances of success and ask yourself, "Why bother?" If everyone thought that way, nobody would ever hit the jackpot in the lottery, win a gold medal at the Olympics or become a successful novelist.

The prospect of a prize or goal, however remote, can drive you forward, but it isn't necessarily the be-all and end-all. Often, the journey is at least as rewarding as the actual achievement.

I know two people, each of whom spent months of their lives writing a novel, only to have it rejected by publisher after publisher. It's hardly surprising – the chance of getting your first novel published is often quoted as about 100 to 1 against.

Yet neither of my friends regrets the time they spent researching and writing their books, because they encountered so many creative challenges and so much stimulation. Both could share their work with others, even if it was as a photocopied manuscript rather than a bound book. And both had that refreshing "take a chance" attitude.

YOU'VE GOT TO BE IN IT TO WIN IT

State lotteries often tempt players by stressing the benefits of "taking a chance", as in the British National Lottery slogan, "You've got to be in it to win it" or the state of Virginia's "You never know." These lines are persuasive, even though the chance of winning the jackpot is minutely small. I don't advocate entering the lottery, but slogans like these can give you the impetus to follow through on any creative project.

CHAPTER 3

THINKING AROUND A PROBLEM

Answering a different question 52

A child's-eye view 54

Simple questions 56

Starting at the end 59

Listening to your daydreams 60

Comparing and contrasting 62

Reversing a problem 65

Lateral thinking exercises 68

The term "lateral thinking" was invented by Edward de Bono in the 1960s and has entered our language. But what does it mean? Is it the same as creative thinking?

The word "lateral" suggests a sideways leap, and while you'll come across different definitions, I find it helpful to distinguish lateral thinking from creative thinking like this:

Creative thinking is coming up with novel ideas for the problem you're presented with.

Lateral thinking is addressing a totally different question from the problem you're presented with.

This chapter shows you techniques for lateral thinking that can be particularly helpful if you feel trapped by a seemingly insoluble difficulty. You'll discover ways to see the issue from another perspective, re-define it in a different form, or even bypass the problem altogether.

ANSWERING A DIFFERENT QUESTION

If you've come up against a problem that seems too big, awkward or expensive to solve, try using lateral thinking. First, look at the problem in the form of a question. Then consider if you're actually asking the right question – or whether you can re-frame your problem as a different question, with a possible answer.

THE PROBLEM THAT DISAPPEARED

According to office legend, there was once a company whose headquarters were in a tall building. Unfortunately, the elevators were extremely slow and staff began to complain about having to wait so long. Then the building manager came up with a brilliant solution. He installed mirrors outside the elevators, and the problem went away.

Why? Instead of pacing around waiting, staff now spent their time using the mirrors to smarten up their appearance – tying ties, adjusting make-up and so on. Their complaints about the elevators stopped.

FROM IMPASSE TO BYPASS

The story given in the box above is often quoted as an example of lateral thinking. The original problem – how to make the elevators go faster – was never solved. Instead, the building manager solved a different problem: how to keep people occupied while they wait.

You can apply the principle of answering a different question to any problem you like, in any area of life. For example, if you're facing a work-related headache such as "How to reduce my costs this year," you could instead address the re-framed, lateral problem "How to increase my revenue this year."

You can also apply lateral thinking to everyday life. For example, I recently had a problem with a tree in the garden of an empty house next door, which was blocking the light in my garden. My problem was "How to contact the elusive landlord" so that I could gain access to the tree through his house. Then it occurred to me that the tree was just as accessible by ladder from my own garden. I didn't need to address the original problem – I could bypass it altogether.

THE "HOW TO" TECHNIQUE

This technique will help you cast a new light on stubborn problems and come up with different answers. Once you've redefined the problem and come up with new ideas, your solutions might seem obvious, yet they can seem ingenious to anyone who's trapped into thinking that they have to solve the original problem.

- Start by stating the basic problem, in the form "How to … "
- Now ask two questions: "*Why* is this a problem?" and "*What's stopping me* from solving it?"
- The answers to these questions will reveal associated problems, each of which you can also list as a "How to". In the elevator example, alternative "How to" statements would include "How to stop people complaining about the elevator," "How to find another way up the building while the elevator is being replaced," or "How to avoid the need to use the elevator when I have a meeting."
- For each "How to" in your list, think about how you might solve it.

A CHILD'S-EYE VIEW

Children have a fresh perspective on the world, which is one thing that makes them so creative. If you're trying to find a new approach to a complex situation, think how you'd explain it to a young child. What pictures would you use to illustrate it? How would you explain it in a way that they'd understand? How could you turn the problem into a story?

CALLING IN THE "CONSULTANTS"

I sometimes run an exercise for senior executives where I tell them they're about to meet some of the most creative consultants they've ever encountered. These consultants, I tell them, are encouraged to use their imagination, have a constant desire to explore and experiment, and have no qualms about offering their own, radical ideas for solving the world's problems.

Then the "consultants" walk into the room. They are, of course, seven-year-old children. Each executive has to explain to the children their job and a problem they're trying to solve, and the children draw pictures and offer ideas for solving the problem.

The children's ideas are likely to be naïve and simplistic, but that's exactly what gives some of them so much impact. Sometimes it takes a child to point out what adults are unable or unwilling to see.

Most important of all, the jargon that often infests adult lives is useless with children. Having to return to plain, simple English helps to unclutter the mind, and suddenly the real issues can shine through.

MAKING IT SIMPLE

If you don't know a child to ask for advice, try the following methods. They all involve simplifying a problem so you can reach its essence.

* * * * *

Write down the problem in one short paragraph. Then reduce that paragraph to a sentence of no more than 10 words. Now reduce it to three words. The ultimate challenge is to reduce the problem to one word.

* * *

Explain the problem to somebody for whom it's completely unfamiliar. Then ask them to state the problem back to you. Their version is bound to be simpler. If they get it wrong, explain which part they've misinterpreted, and ask them to state it again.

* * *

Draw the problem as a diagram or picture (or cut and paste images from the web or from a magazine), adding no more than five words for labels or annotations. Pictures can convey complex ideas in a very concise way.

* * *

Don't focus on the problem — imagine what the solution will be, and state that in 10 words. Once you've identified the solution you're looking for, it should be easier to define the problem clearly.

"Life is really simple, but we insist on making it complicated."

Confucius (551–479BC)

SIMPLE QUESTIONS

The previous section looked at children's responses to the world, and one of their favourite responses is "Why?" Often, they like this one so much they repeat it again and again. Doing the same can inspire you to think laterally. Other very basic questions, such as "Who?" and "What?", can help you enlarge and refine your ideas.

I keep six honest serving-men
(They taught me all I knew);
Their names are What and Why and When
And How and Where and Who.

Rudyard Kipling (1865–1936)

KEEP ASKING "WHY?"

You aren't limited to asking "Why?" once. You can keep on asking, to help you get to the root of an issue. The "Why? Why?" technique has been a popular tool for problem-solving on factory floors for years.

I can recall an occasion that showed how easy it is to become bogged down in the detail of a problem; and, equally, how easy it can be to get out of your difficulty. I was part of a large group organizing a conference for teachers, and we were trying to decide on a date. It had been decided that the conference should run from Friday to Monday around Easter time, but some of us were worried that too few people would attend on the final day.

Eventually we found a solution, but we could have found it so much earlier if we'd simply applied the "Why? Why?" technique right at the start. Our thinking went something like this:

We need to find ways to boost attendance on the final day of the conference.

Why?

Because most people we've spoken to won't be able to make it that day.

Why?

Because it's a Monday, when teachers work.

Why does the conference have to finish on a Monday?

Because the conference is four days long and needs to include a weekend.

This process could have continued for several more stages, with each "Because" generating ideas. In fact, the solution came from the third Why, "Why does the conference have to finish on a Monday?" Instead of running from Friday to Monday, we simply moved the conference to run from Thursday to Sunday. Like many "out of the box" solutions, this one seemed obvious after the event. Yet when you're focusing on the minutiae, such solutions can seem like a flash of inspiration.

... AND WHO, WHAT, WHERE, WHEN AND HOW?

Asking "Why?" is a way of opening a problem up. The five other questions – "Who?", "What?", "Where?", "When?" and "How?" – are ways to help you get stuck into the practicalities, but they can also encourage you to think laterally and generate further ideas about the problem. These simple questions all help you to bring relevant issues out into the open, and the mere act of articulating every aspect of the issue can often suggest different points of entry.

The box below gives some examples of each type of question, showing how they can reveal particular aspects of a problem. As you can see in most of the examples, the main questions might easily lead on to associated questions, which can eventually point you in the direction of new ideas and possible solutions.

WHO	is part of the problem? ... Are there any other people I can involve?
WHAT	is the problem? What are the constraints stopping me from acting? What objects or ideas could I do without? What else could I use?
WHERE	am I planning to solve the problem? ... Why not do it somewhere else?
WHEN	am I planning to address the problem? ... Why not do something about it sooner, or later?
HOW	am I going about tackling the problem? ... Is there another way?

STARTING AT THE END

We all have dreams of where we'd like to be or what we'd like to do in life, and part of the reason why people want to be creative is to realize those dreams. You can begin to fire up your imagination by starting with those aspirations.

IMAGINE YOU'VE DONE IT …

Whatever your goal, picture yourself reaching it. Once you've imagined your successful self, start to work backward. Ask yourself how you got there. What was the final step? And the one before that? By tracking back all the way, you can create a plan for getting to your destination.

To bring this concept to life, you might imagine yourself in a particular situation, such as being interviewed by a journalist about your achievement. She might ask questions like the following:

- "What part of the project did you enjoy the most?"
- "How do you feel now that you've achieved your goal?"
- "What are people saying to you?"
- "How has your life got better?"
- "What possibilities has this success opened up for you?"
- "What was the biggest challenge that you faced? How did you get around it?"
- "Was this enterprise difficult for your friends and family?"

This approach can help to give you new insights into what your real priorities are, and which problems are the most important to tackle.

LISTENING TO YOUR DAYDREAMS

Daydreaming can be distracting – but it's wonderful for your creative thinking, and you should nurture it, not fight it. Listen to your inner voice. It's the voice that asks "What if …?", and wistfully ponders "If only …" and "I wish …" These thoughts can help to unlock new ideas.

SETTING YOUR MIND FREE

When you're reading or listening to new information, your mind tends to drift off every so often. While the logical part of the brain takes in facts and deciphers the language, the intuitive part goes off at a tangent, asking questions and making connections. Both processes are necessary, giving you the knowledge and ideas to tackle problems.

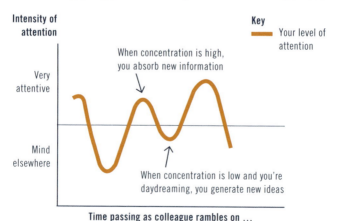

Intensity of attention

Key
━━━ Your level of attention

Very attentive

Mind elsewhere

When concentration is high, you absorb new information

When concentration is low and you're daydreaming, you generate new ideas

Time passing as colleague rambles on …

THE "I WISH" TECHNIQUE

The words "I wish …" let you break free of all your constraints for a little while. This freedom can be a simple way to help you get past a point where you're stuck.

* * * * *

Start by defining your problem or goal. Imagine you're talking to a friend and just let your ideas flow. Look for brief answers to the questions:

"What's the problem?"

"What's getting in the way?"

"What have I tried already?"

It helps to record your description in writing or onto a mini tape recorder.

Give yourself a short rest, then read or listen to your description. As you do so, let your mind drift, and write down what you hope or wish to happen, starting each statement with the words "I wish". Set yourself a target of at least ten I-wishes. You can wish for anything you want – even for the impossible, or for a problem to go away.

Use these I-wishes as a starting point for a fresh look at your problem.

It can be better to do this exercise with a friend – one of you describes the problem and the other records their I-wishes.

COMPARING AND CONTRASTING

The French author Madame de Staël once commented: "Wit consists in knowing the resemblance of things which differ, and the difference of things which are alike." This idea could just as well apply to creativity. Comparing and contrasting can give you a fresh insight into familiar situations.

LOOK FOR CONNECTIONS

The brain is naturally good at spotting connections, and you can improve this ability with practice. Take two seemingly unrelated items at random from an encyclopedia, and see how many similarities you can find between them. For example, I picked out the following words:

VITAMINS   PHOTOGRAPHS

At first glance, these two items have no connections or similarities at all. But if you think about it …
- **Both** are things that you "take" …
- … and people generally take far more than they need!
- **Both** require chemical processes to make them.
- **Both** are sold at pharmacies.
- **Both** are words with three syllables.

You can apply this way of thinking to other apparently unconnected situations, to help you find new approaches to a problem.

THE CONNECTIONS TEST

If you ever find yourself facing a new problem and saying, "This situation has nothing in common with anything I've done before," challenge yourself to the connections test.

* * * * *

Briefly describe the problem you're trying to solve. For example: "How to get the kids to help with household chores."

* * *

Next, turn this particular issue into a general problem, such as: "How to get the kids to do something they don't want to do" or even: "How to get people to do something they don't want to do."

* * *

Think about other situations where this general problem has arisen. "Getting people to do something they don't want to do" applies in all sorts of situations – for example, asking squeamish people to give blood or getting drivers to stay inside the speed limit.

* * *

Think how these other problems are solved, and how you can adapt those solutions for your own situation.

To get people to give blood, you might show the good it does for others – or even themselves. You could say to your children that keeping the house tidy helps them find things and gives you more time with them.

To get drivers to slow down, we have signs that clearly state the speed limit. You could have a notice board showing jobs for each child (vacuum the living room, fold the laundry) and gold stars when they've done it.

A DIFFERENT PERSPECTIVE

If you constantly find yourself up against the "same old" problem, ask yourself what's different this time. As the saying goes, "If you always do what you always did, you'll always get what you always got." Even a small change can help you break the pattern. A simple yet effective way to make this change is to try someone else's approach.

One of the many successful, if painful, reality TV shows of recent years has been the programme *Wife Swap*, in which two housewives exchange lives for two weeks. For one week they get to impose their rules on their new household, and for the second week they have to live by the other wife's rules. In the interests of "good TV", the exchanges are typically between people of completely contrasting values and lifestyles, and often end in a shouting match.

Nevertheless, temporarily living the life of another person – trying their job, living in their community, socializing with their friends or even just doing their shopping – could reveal as much about your way of thinking as it does about theirs. You might pick up lots of ideas from their different way of dealing with everyday tasks.

If this idea appeals to you, try the following steps:

- **Ask yourself: who could you swap with for a week?**
  A neighbour? A relative in another country? One of your children?
- **Keep it simple.**
  A complete lifestyle swap might be too complicated, so you could just pick out certain activities instead. Exchange recipes and try cooking the other person's favourite food. Watch a favourite movie of theirs that you've never seen.

REVERSING A PROBLEM

Another way to break out from a tough problem is to turn it back to front. At first sight, this technique seems absurd, but looking at the opposite of the problem can give surprising insights and perfectly sensible solutions.

LESS HASTE, MORE SPEED

To take one example, how do you get cars to go faster on a congested road? It turns out that one effective solution is to make them go slower. This idea sounds like a riddle from *Alice in Wonderland*, but the explanation is quite logical. When cars are going fast, drivers have less reaction time and are prone to sudden braking, which can bring the traffic to a standstill. If cars are given a speed restriction of, say, 40mph, traffic moves more steadily and, like the tortoise versus the hare in Aesop's fable, people can arrive sooner at their destination.

THE EXPANDING TROLLEY

The reversal technique was used to good effect by a designer trying to create a smaller catering trolley for use on an aircraft (so people could squeeze past in the aisles). In search of inspiration, he considered the reverse problem, "how to make the trolley larger." His solution for a larger trolley was to run it on rails above the corridor (the only place where it would fit). If the trolley was larger, he could fit ovens inside to heat the food, and in turn the kitchen could be smaller so they could squeeze more seats into the plane. This idea turned out to be feasible and was subsequently patented.

WHY DOES REVERSING WORK?

This technique works because it's an immediate, deliberate way of challenging your assumptions. Even if it fails to give you practical solutions, it can still help you to gain a new perspective on the problem that you're tackling.

The other advantage of the reversal technique is that it makes the problem more fun. There's something appealing to the human psyche about doing the opposite of what we're supposed to do. Turning a problem upside down can also make it easier for you to generate ideas. For example, if you're struggling to save money, try thinking up outrageous ways to spend it instead. Your choices might reveal the temptations that prompt you to buy things you don't need.

USING THE TECHNIQUE

When you're driving a car and you go down a dead end, you need your reverse gear to get you out. You can think of the reversing technique in the same way – helping you to explore different avenues when your way forward seems to be blocked. You can use the technique for just about any problem, at work or at home. Here are a couple of examples:

Sending out greeting cards

Instead of worrying about how to send out greeting cards earlier this year, think about how you can send them all later.
When you're sending out cards for an end-of-year festival such as Christmas, if you mail them later than normal they might not reach people until the end of the year – which suggests the idea of sending

New Year cards instead. It's not such a crazy idea: nobody has time to read all their cards and letters before Christmas anyway, so your communication might have more impact if you delay it.

Taking your children to soccer practice
Instead of wondering how you can deliver the kids to soccer practice, think about how to get them to deliver *you*.
What could this mean? You could take it literally – get them to hook a trailer onto their bikes and tow you. But there are more practical ways to interpret the challenge. Maybe, instead of chasing around to get the kids ready, you could change the emphasis to having them sort out what has to be done before you can go out. Allow yourself to be very loose in how you interpret the word "deliver".

MULTI-WAY REVERSING
There's usually more than one way to reverse a problem. So "How to get a new job" could become "How to stay in my existing job" or "How to get an *old* job" (this might mean going back to one of *your* old jobs) or "How to make a new job get *me*." Each statement points you in a different direction for possible ideas.

Similarly, if you're looking for a new home, "How to find a suitable place to live that I can afford" could become "How to find an unsuitable place I can afford" (maybe you'll find it's not so bad after all), "How to find a suitable place that I *can't* afford" (and then find a way of affording it), or "How to stop trying to find a suitable place" (stay where I am and let fate deliver something to me).

LATERAL THINKING EXERCISES

Puzzles involving lateral thinking can be a quick, effective
way to stretch your mind, as well as being fun. The exercises
here challenge your visual and logical powers. (The solutions
are on pages 137–8.) How far out of the box can you go?

BREAKING OUT AGAIN

In the nine-dot puzzle on page 8 of this book, you were set the
challenge of finding a way to connect all the dots using only four
straight lines, without your pen leaving the paper. In fact, it's possible
to solve this puzzle using three lines – and there's more than way of
doing it with only one. Can you find them, without breaking the rules?

There's a less well-known version of this puzzle, involving 16 dots:
see next page, top. You have to put at least one line through each dot,
without lifting your pen from the paper, using only six lines in all. The
16-dot puzzle has at least 10 solutions, not counting "trick" answers.
Once you know the solution to the nine-dot puzzle, it should take only
a few minutes to find one solution to the 16-dot puzzle. Finding others
takes longer, and for some you have to think a long way out of the box.

PUZZLING QUESTIONS

As a further test of your reasoning and lateral thinking abilities, you might like to try the following brain-teasers. The solutions can be found on page 138.

Question 1

If you check the statistics, you'll find that Canadians eat less in February than in any other month.

Why is this?

Question 2

"How old are you?" Stan asked Sally. "A couple of days ago I was 12," Sally replied, "but next year I'll be 15."

How can this be possible?

Question 3

In the following sequence of letters, which letter comes next?

OTTFFSS

INTERLUDE
THE MESSINESS OF CREATIVITY

Otto von Bismarck once said: "People who love sausage and respect the law should never watch either being made." Much the same principle applies to innovation. We tend to see creativity as a flash of inspiration leading to a brilliant result. What we rarely see is the messy process of getting there — the blind alleys, arguments and hopeless prototypes. Here are some of my favourite examples.

SYDNEY OPERA HOUSE

The Sydney Opera House, by the Danish architect Jørn Utzen, has become one of Australia's greatest icons, and the view of the Opera House with the Harbour Bridge as a backdrop is one of the most photogenic in the world. Yet its design and construction became, for a while, a source of ridicule and embarrassment.

The idea was simple and beautiful: to have a building reminiscent of a tall sailing ship passing through the harbour. The original design had interlocking roofs, much as we see today — but each roof had a complex curved shape, which made tiling them hugely difficult and expensive. It was only when somebody thought of shaping the roofs as segments of a sphere that the problem was solved.

Massive overspending, compromises and last-minute design changes all plagued the project. Yet when the Opera House was finished, 16 years after starting, the public forgave everything, and people around the world have loved it ever since.

THE DISCOVERY OF DRUGS

The history of drug development is riddled with accidental discoveries and neglect. The most famous example is penicillin. The Scottish biologist Alexander Fleming returned to his lab one morning to discover that some dirt had blown through the window and killed the bacteria he was cultivating. The invading substance was a mould called *Penicillium notatum*. What is less well known is that this accident happened in 1928 – more than 13 years before the first successful treatment of a human patient.

The discovery lay dormant because Fleming didn't regard it as having much practical use. It took hard work, ingenious insights, and trial and error by other scientists in England and America before penicillin could be produced in significant quantities for medical use.

Nitrous oxide, one of the first anesthetics, has a similar history. The gas was discovered in 1795, but was used just for entertainment, as a laughing gas, for the next 50 years. One night, at a laughing-gas demonstration, a volunteer who tried it was found to have gashed his leg and not felt anything. By chance, the man who noticed this effect was a dentist, who immediately thought of a good application.

YESTERDAY, AND OTHER LYRICS

Once a song has entered the pop charts, its words become part of our culture, never to be changed. It's easy to forget that songs are like any other creative work, and go through numerous changes and revisions before they're set in their final form.

Most songs start as a fragment of an idea. Paul McCartney has told how he woke up with the tune for the song "Yesterday" in his head. In the absence of any lyrics, he decided to call it "Scrambled Eggs" — words that fit the rhythm, but certainly don't have the sound of a smash hit about them.

Tim Rice has documented how the lyrics for *Evita*, the concept album that became a world-famous musical, went through countless redrafts as the deadline for producing the album approached. Do you recognize the song whose opening line, in one early draft, was: "All through my reckless and wild days," and in another was "It's only your lover returning"? Both of these lines were scrapped at the last minute, in favour of the line "Don't cry for me, Argentina."

POST-IT® NOTES

Today, Post-It® notes are a familiar sight in our offices and homes. It seems incredible that something so useful took so long to appear.

In 1968, Spencer Silver, a chemist working for the 3M corporation, discovered a very weak adhesive. Searching for a use for this product, 3M developed the Post-It® bulletin board, which had a sticky surface so that people didn't need to use thumb-tacks. It was not a success.

The next idea came from Art Fry, a researcher at 3M. Sitting in church one day, he got frustrated that the bits of paper he was using as bookmarks in a hymnal kept slipping out, and had the idea for slightly sticky bookmarks, using the 3M glue. He tested the idea at work, but there was little demand. Some time later, Fry had his second flash of inspiration – to scribble a message on a sticky note and fix it to a document. Now the idea became popular. Even so, he met resistance from the company and a lack of interest from the public. However, so many people at 3M believed this idea was good that they gave it another launch in 1980, this time as the Post-It® note.

The same themes occur time and again: the value of many innovations is recognized only after the event, and the creative process can be arduous and filled with uncertainty. If that's how your project feels, then take heart – you could still be on to something big.

CHAPTER 4

GENERATING IDEAS

Where do ideas come from? 76

Warming up your mind 78

Patterns of thought 80

Doing something totally different 82

Seeking a second opinion 83

Inspirational people 84

Bending reality 86

Figuratively speaking 90

Old idea + old idea = new idea 92

Storing ideas 95

Serendipity 96

When words collide 98

Picking a theme 101

Having a Plan B 103

The previous chapter was about ways to get around a problem. But sometimes you can't avoid the issue, and you've simply got to come up with ideas. This is where you might feel stuck. You need to choose where to go on vacation? All you can think of is the same places you've been before. You have to write a speech? You can't get beyond the opening line.

Most people strive to think up "good" ideas straight away, and then look through those ideas in the hope that one of them might be original. If you want to break out of the box, sometimes it's better to work the other way around: first look for original ideas and then see if you can adapt them for your purposes. In this chapter, we'll look at ways to inspire new ideas, by tapping into the world around you or by deliberately giving your mind a jolt.

WHERE DO IDEAS COME FROM?

Certain situations provide fertile ground for ideas. If you know what they are, you can take steps to create them. That way, you can more easily come up with an idea when you want one, rather than having to wait for inspiration to strike.

TRIGGERS FOR IDEAS

What is it that causes an idea to pop into your head? Generally, you're most likely to come up with ideas in the following circumstances:

Having a reason to generate ideas

You're unlikely to have ideas if you don't have a reason for them. Until the mid-1990s, few people used the worldwide web, because hardly anyone knew that it existed. Today, millions of people have their own website. Put yourself in new situations that could trigger ideas.

Necessity – the mother of invention

Do you know how to build your own home and live off the land? If you suddenly found yourself stuck on a desert island, you'd have no choice but to learn! Ideas flow when you need them, so facing – or even creating – a crisis is one way of ensuring that you come up with them.

Being fed up with how things are

Feeling dissatisfied with a situation is a strong trigger for ideas. For example, in 19th-century London, open sewers discharging into the

Thames made many areas smell foul. The politicians did little until "The Big Stink" in the summer of 1858, when the smell from the Thames became so noxious that the Houses of Parliament closed. Suddenly everyone had ideas on how to solve the problem. The result was the sewerage system that survives to this day.

Seeing somebody else's idea

Ideas spread through communities like a virus. If one trend-setter builds a deck in their backyard, suddenly everyone wants one. The more you see of how other people invent things or solve problems, the more ideas you're likely to find for your own situation.

Being "ripe"

Sources for ideas are all around us, but for those ideas to leap out, we often need to be in a state of mind that the philosopher Arthur Koestler described as "ripe". He noted that the more immersed people were in a problem, the more likely they'd be ripe for having ideas.

A KNOTTY PROBLEM

In the 1940s, Swiss engineer George de Mestrel started wondering how to create a better way to fasten clothing when the zip fastener on his wife's dress got stuck one day. Months later, when out walking in the mountains, he spotted burrs clinging to his dog's coat. The burrs turned out to have tiny hooks, which were snagging on loops of the dog's hair. Because de Mestrel's mind was ripe for an idea about fasteners, he came up with the hook-and-loop concept of Velcro®.

WARMING UP YOUR MIND

Before a match or a competition, sportsmen get themselves ready with a warm-up. Creative thinkers can do the same. If you're feeling uninspired or tired, an activity to energize your mind, or a diversion, can make a big difference.

INSTANT ENERGIZERS

The following tips can provide an immediate boost if you feel your mental or physical energy is flagging:

- **Physical activity**
  Getting up and pacing around, or going for a walk or a jog, can click your brain into another gear. The activity gets your circulation going, making you more alert, and the change of scene will stimulate your mind.

- **Stimulating music**
  Much has been made of the "Mozart effect", in which listening to Mozart is said to enhance your thinking skills. However, the music doesn't have to be Mozart – it could be rock music or a pop song. Listen to energizing music that works for you.

- **Humour**
  Creative thinking and laughter are closely linked. One reason why we laugh is because we've heard something that doesn't fit our normal view of the world; in the same way, creative ideas are ones that overturn our expectations. If you're feeling bereft of ideas, find something or someone to make you laugh.

STIMULATING MIND GAMES

Games and puzzles are another ideal way to prepare your mind for creative thinking. You might like to try the following suggestions, either by yourself or with friends.

* * * * *

Alone or with others
Imagine the first line of a book
Look for a book that you haven't read. Try to guess the opening line before opening the book.

What will tomorrow's headlines be?
It's often easy to predict what the main news story will be in tomorrow's papers, but what will the headlines be? Listen to TV and radio news, and try creating a pithy headline of your own before you see the real thing.

* * *

Games for groups
Two truths and a lie
Each of you secretly writes down two things that have happened to you and one that you've made up. Then you each read out your lists; everyone has to guess which item is the lie. The skill is in inventing plausible lies.

Invent a definition
Take it in turns to find an obscure word in a dictionary. Everyone writes down a definition, and puts it into a hat. The true definition is also put in. Each definition is read out. You score points if you guess the correct one, or if somebody thinks your invented definition is the real one.

PATTERNS OF THOUGHT

You can help ideas to flow simply by getting your first few down on paper. However, ideas don't usually come in a nice, logical order, but may appear from all directions. If you put them down in a list, they can seem unconnected. They may make more sense if you try showing them as a diagram.

MAKING A SPIDER DIAGRAM

One way of structuring your ideas is to use a spider diagram (more technically known as a semantic map). An example is shown opposite.

Write the central theme for your ideas (for example: "Thank-you gift for Aunt Maggie") in the middle of a page – this will be the "body" of the spider. Write associated ideas around the page and then draw lines connecting them to the body, to form the "legs". You can give your "spider" any number of legs. Each one can branch out into other legs as you subdivide categories and as different ideas pop up.

The advantage of this technique is that it draws your ideas out in multiple directions, rather than the single direction of a list. It also allows you to connect ideas by association, which mimics the way that the brain works. It can sometimes almost feel as if the technique is drawing ideas out of you – if an area of the paper is blank, it begs to be filled by a new branch and new ideas.

Fans of this technique don't just use it as a method of generating ideas. They also apply it for recalling information, taking notes or structuring a talk. You can use it in whichever way works for you.

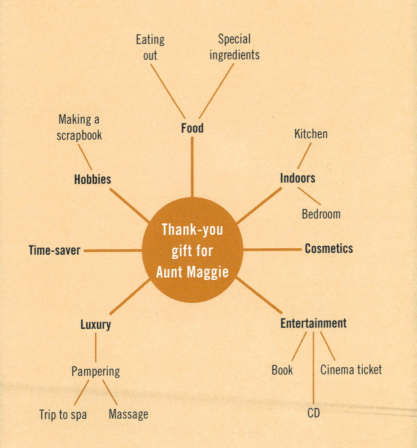

Eating out

Special ingredients

Food

Making a scrapbook

Hobbies

Kitchen

Indoors

Bedroom

Time-saver

Thank-you gift for Aunt Maggie

Cosmetics

Luxury

Pampering

Trip to spa

Massage

Entertainment

Book

Cinema ticket

CD

DOING SOMETHING TOTALLY DIFFERENT

I once asked a composer from New York how he created a new piece of music. Did he take a blank sheet and wait for ideas? Not at all: he said that ideas only came when he was doing something else completely. This answer is typical of many creative professionals – and it could help you, too.

USEFUL DISTRACTIONS

The best type of distraction is a mundane task that needs some concentration. For the composer, that might be sorting papers or research, but it could also be non-musical, such as mowing the lawn. You could try a household chore, or a fiddly activity such as doing a jigsaw puzzle. The inventor Thomas Edison liked to go fishing. He had no intention of catching fish: he simply wanted time to himself.

IDEAS IN UNLIKELY PLACES

The fact that ideas can appear from just about anywhere was noted by psychologist Wolfgang Köhler. A Scottish physicist once told him: "We often talk about the Three B's: the Bus, the Bath, and the Bed. That's where the great discoveries are made in our science."

First, immerse yourself in your challenge. For example, write down your objectives or do some research. Now give up for a while. The time you spent on the task will help you define your aims and any problems. The distraction will help your unconscious mind turn up new ideas.

SEEKING A SECOND OPINION

Creative thinking is usually seen as a solitary activity. However, this lonely approach doesn't work for everyone: indeed, it can lead to mental blocks. You can lose a sense of perspective and your thinking can become stale. Therefore, one highly effective way to help you build your own ideas is to find somebody to share them with.

TWO HEADS CAN BE BETTER THAN ONE

The British educationalist Graham Wallas (1858–1932) showed the benefits of having a "sounding board" in his book *The Art of Thought*. He quotes a little girl who, when told to be sure what she meant before she spoke, said, "How can I know what I think until I see what I say?"

Take care whom you choose as a confidant. More than anything, you need a good listener. Being able to explain your ideas without someone interrupting or laughing at you can help you to form and refine them. You might already know what it's like to tell somebody about an idea, receive only understanding nods in response, and at the end find yourself saying, "Thanks. That really helped!"

It also helps to be questioned. There are bound to be things you haven't considered, and somebody who's unfamiliar with the issue will ask testing questions, so they can understand. A second mind can also bring a fresh perspective and build on your concepts. This person doesn't need to be full of ideas to offer an inspiring new angle. There are more tips about being creative with other people in Chapter 5.

INSPIRATIONAL PEOPLE

Famous people, particularly those whom you admire, can be a source of inspiration for ideas. You can follow their example by looking at their attitudes and achievements. You can also use famous people's characters as a way of role-playing different ways to tackle problems.

A DIRECTOR'S HERO

Billy Wilder was one of the greatest directors of all time, with movies such as *Some Like It Hot* and *Sunset Boulevard*. Wilder has been an inspiration for many other directors, but he too had his own source of inspiration – the early, innovative director Ernst Lubitsch. On his office wall hung a sign saying: "How would Ernst Lubitsch have done it?"

WHO ARE YOUR IDOLS?

As the story of Billy Wilder shows, even the most successful people have figures they admire. Our image of these idols is almost always distorted: we want to hear about their best features, not their frailties. Hero worship can be taken too far, of course, but in moderation everyone can be helped by having a role model who encapsulates the qualities to which they aspire.

Whose influence would you like to tap into? What is it about him or her that you admire? Put up a picture of that person in a visible place – above your computer, on the refrigerator, on the rear window of your car – and use it as a constant reminder. Or simply copy Wilder by putting up the phrase, "How would [my idol] have done it?"

GETTING HELP FROM YOUR HEROES

Instead of fretting about how you're going to solve a problem, put yourself in the mind of a famous achiever or problem-solver, or a fictional character. For example, imagine you're looking for a way to stop people spraying graffiti on walls. Here's how three famous names might approach the problem – it's a simplistic view of these characters, but might provide food for thought.

- **John Lennon** might, in his famous words, "Give Peace a Chance" and reason with the offenders – or he might make the walls into Peace" walls, allowing graffiti with friendly, non-violent themes.
- **Dorothy** (from *The Wizard of Oz*) might get all emotional, using tears to pull on the heartstrings, make the offenders feel guilty, and show them how their damage is affecting other people.
- **Sherlock Holmes** would look clinically at the evidence, detecting where graffiti artists were getting their materials and when they committed their offences, as well as discovering more subtle motives than those that the bumbling police force worked out.

ACHIEVERS AND PROBLEM-SOLVERS

Each person and character below has a particular mindset. By borrowing from that mindset you can open up different avenues for ideas.

Clark Kent/Superman	Winston Churchill	Nelson Mandela
Cary Grant	Stephen Hawking	Oprah Winfrey
Audrey Hepburn	Madonna	Bill Gates
Lara Croft	Tiger Woods	Marge Simpson

BENDING REALITY

In the "What If?" game on page 40, you have to think beyond the bounds of normality. You can apply this technique to situations where you're trying to think creatively, by exploring what would happen if you changed the conditions.

WHAT IF THIS WERE DIFFERENT?

The simplest way to expand your horizons is to ask: "What if this were different?" This question can be one of the most inspiring. It opens up hundreds of ways to tackle an issue, because there are so many aspects of the problem that you could change.

The technique can be illustrated with the following example. Suppose you wanted to design a new type of train. To make it interesting, let's say it's a tourist train that runs through spectacular scenery. You might not think there's much to be creative about. But as with any situation, you don't know what interesting ideas might emerge until you explore with an open mind.

The first step in the "What if this were different?" technique is to write down everything you can think of about how things are now, no matter how obvious. For the train, the list might begin like this:

- The locomotive is at the front, pulling the train.
- The train driver sits in the locomotive.
- Passengers sit in seats.
- Passengers look out of the windows at the scenery.
- The train travels on tracks.

For each item in the list, you can now ask, "What if this were different?" and then let your mind explore.

"The locomotive is at the front ... "
What if this were different?

Locomotives don't have to go at the front – trains are sometimes pushed from the rear. If the loco isn't at the front, then a passenger carriage could go at the front instead.

Wouldn't it be great if the front carriage could be an observation car, with fantastic views out of the front window? But there might be a problem with safety – doesn't the train driver need to be able to see the tracks? This leads on to the next item in the list.

"The train driver sits in the locomotive."
What if this were different?

Is it possible for the train driver not to sit inside the locomotive? Of course, this arrangement already exists in airplanes, where the pilot sits at the front, a long way from the engines.

In our train, we could have the driver in a raised capsule, an observation car with panoramic windows beneath, and the main locomotive in the middle or rear. If this idea sounds a bit off the wall, you might like to know that a train like this already exists – the Crystal Panoramic Express, which runs through the Swiss Alps.

This idea has emerged just by exploring two items in our list. Imagine how many ideas you could generate from a list of 100 items.

FURTHER "WHAT IF?" QUESTIONS

"What if it were different?" is a very open question, because you could start anywhere. There are more specific ways in which you can bend reality to get your thinking going.

What if you could magically remove the constraints?

Coming up with ideas is a struggle if there's a stack of rules and demands to overcome. Instead of looking for ideas that meet these criteria, free yourself by forgetting the constraints for a while.

I once worked with a team who had to create a giveaway item for a conference in the Netherlands. However, the item had to be cheaper than $10, it had to have a Dutch theme, it had to be a game, it had to be something that would appeal to everyone, and it had to tie in with the theme of the conference. All those constraints stifled us, so we simply tried to think of a game with a Dutch theme. Now the ideas flowed. (One was a variant of pinning the tail on the donkey: "pinning the ear on Van Gogh". It wasn't used, but it gave us a good laugh.)

Some more ideas to try:
- What if you did things in a different order?
- What if money were no object?
- What if this were being done in Japan?
- What if it were 100 times smaller?
- What if it had to be done by tonight?
- What if you stopped trying to tackle it?
- What if you were the object you're making? How would you feel?

TAKING AN IDEA TO THE LIMIT

Exaggeration is fun! It can also help you to break through barriers to your thinking. Let's say you're looking at ways to advertise a sale at your children's school. Your thoughts might follow a pattern like this – growing more outrageous, then coming down to a practical solution.

How can you tell all the parents?

Exaggerate the idea

Why just parents? Why not the whole town?

Why not everyone within 100 miles?

WHY NOT GET ONTO NATIONAL TV NEWS?

How can you apply these ideas to your sale?

SALE AT YOUR SCHOOL

OUTRAGEOUS!

The criteria can apply at local as well as national level

Tell a human-interest story

Link it to a celebrity

Break a record

SO HOW DO YOU GET AN ITEM INTO THE NEWS?

FIGURATIVELY SPEAKING

Our language is greatly enriched by using figures of speech, such as similes or analogies, to describe situations. By finding just the right expression to describe a task or problem that you're facing, you can create a more vivid picture of it, and perhaps find new insights and ideas.

WHAT DOES IT FEEL LIKE?

Figures of speech can range from the sublime, such as Wordsworth's "I wandered lonely as a cloud," to the ridiculous, like Homer Simpson's pearl of wisdom, "A boy without mischief is like a bowling ball without a liquid center." To describe your situation, you could use anything from well-known sayings to ones that you've just made up.

For example, have another look at the problem described on page 63: trying to get your children to do jobs around the house. You could start by asking: "What does it feel like trying to get them to work?" You might come up with familiar comparisons such as these:

- "It's like pulling teeth!"
- "It's like wading through syrup!"
- "It's like trying to push water uphill!"

Each of these analogies creates a clear picture of the frustrations involved, which can be extremely useful if you want to communicate your thoughts to somebody else. You can also take them further, to help you find possible solutions.

- **"Like pulling teeth"**

  You're tugging hard and getting howls of protest, but nothing is giving way. How would a dentist get around this problem? He or she might give a general anesthetic so the patient doesn't notice the pain. Perhaps you could apply an "anesthetic" by turning the housework into a game with points, so your children don't notice how boring it is.

- **"Like wading through syrup"**

  Progress is slow, and you're meeting a lot of resistance. What is the low-energy way of motivating your children? To speak calmly and reasonably instead of shouting? To ask the children to help in family areas, but let them make as much mess as they like in their bedrooms? A more cunning plan might be to apply pressure on a weak spot. For example, you could pay them to do a task if they want extra spending money.

- **"Like trying to push water uphill"**

  You're making no headway at all, and your children keep slipping back to where they started. So how would you push water uphill? One way might be to pump it through a leak-proof device or system so there's nowhere else for the water to go. To stop your children's attention leaking away, you could remove other sources of distraction, so they have to focus on the task in hand.

You could try applying these expressions to your problem, find more unusual ones (such as "It's like trying to dig a hole in the sea!") or make up your own — the funnier, the better.

OLD IDEA + OLD IDEA = NEW IDEA

Few of us have truly original ideas, but we can easily come up with new ideas by combining old ones. As choreographer Twyla Tharp put it, "Nothing's really original. Not Homer or Shakespeare and certainly not you. Get over it."

MIXING AND MATCHING

All new ideas are, in a way, a re-combination of old patterns – yet that doesn't stop the result from being exciting. Music is a good example. Oasis, one of the most successful rock groups of recent times, drew heavily on ideas from the Beatles. The Beatles, in turn, were inspired by rock and roll, Indian music and medieval church music. Their talent was in combining these influences with modern lyrics and instruments.

You can come up with instant new ideas simply by mixing things that don't normally go together. For example, the box below contains

MAIN FOOD	"NORMAL" PARTNER
Burgers	Barbecue sauce
Beef	Horseradish
Pork	Apple sauce
Chicken	Curry sauce
Bacon	Fried egg
Ice cream	Strawberries
Pancakes	Maple syrup

names of foods that are commonly combined. To create a new meal, pick one item from the left-hand column and one from a different row in the right-hand column.

Ice cream with curry sauce … Pancakes with horseradish … Beef and strawberries … Burgers with maple syrup? That selection will certainly challenge the taste buds. They might sound like a culinary nightmare, but perhaps that's just because you've never tried them. Can you see any new pairs that might actually work?

The Fat Duck restaurant in Bray, southern England – one of the best restaurants in the world – has won three Michelin stars for its innovative meals. The restaurant owner, Heston Blumenthal, combines foods that are normally kept apart. Among the delights that have been served there are bacon and egg ice cream, snail porridge and chocolate with tobacco.

EXISTING COMBINATIONS

In almost any creative field, new ideas can be formed by combining old ones. Many of the results are familiar fixtures in our world, such as shampoo-conditioners or pencils with erasers on the end.

- **Fashion**
  New fashions can simply be a recombination of old ideas. Some designers deliberately borrow from historical sources, like Vivienne Westwood with her creations based on 17th- and 18th-century dresses. At other times, a fashion seems to emerge spontaneously. One example is the idea of wearing dresses over the top of jeans, which briefly spread through Europe and North America in 2005.

- **TV shows**

  Many hit TV shows are a blend of old ideas. On paper, "Vampire horror meets high school comedy" might have looked like a dud, yet it became *Buffy the Vampire Slayer* – a huge TV success. In the world of quiz shows, "Multiple-choice questions meet big cash prizes" became the phenomenal ratings-buster *Who Wants to be a Millionaire?*

- **Technology**

  Many successful technological ideas have come about by combining two everyday functions. Digital clocks and bedside radios had been around for years before somebody had the bright idea of the clock-radio. The petrol (gasoline) car and the electric car were well established long before the idea of a hybrid car, which can be powered by both sources of energy, was conceived.

> **IS IT A PLANE? IS IT A HELICOPTER?**
> A striking example of combined technologies is the V22-Osprey, a military aircraft that has both wings and rotors. The Osprey can take off and land vertically, like a helicopter; it can also swivel its rotors forward and fly like an airplane.

What new concepts can you create by simply combining old ones? Think of two areas where you're trying to come up with ideas, and merge them. "Wedding reception" meets "Garden revamp". "Re-upholstering the sofa" meets "Personal web page". "Getting fit" meets "Vacation in Australia". With combinations like that, you can't help but come up with something new.

STORING IDEAS

It often isn't enough to have a good idea: timing can be crucial as well. Too many good ideas are lost because they appeared at the wrong time and weren't even recorded. Yet your old ideas can be one of the best sources of inspiration.

KEEPING IDEAS ON RECORD

Ideas can pop up in the most inconvenient places: in the bath, while you're driving, or during a sleepless moment at four o'clock in the morning. They can flit away and be lost unless you record them. It pays to start carrying a notebook and pencil, or at least keep notebooks in handy places such as in the car or next to the bed.

Create a file for ideas that you never took anywhere. You can then revisit them for inspiration when your mind is drawing a blank. Sketches, notes scribbled on the back of envelopes and simple prototypes can all be stored.

If you're a meticulous filer, you could keep groups of ideas in separate folders. However, if you're a disorganized sort, like me, then just dump all your jottings into one file. The random jumbling of ideas can be exactly the jolt that your thinking needs at some future date.

"The Possible's slow fuse is lit
By the imagination."

Emily Dickinson (1830–86)

SERENDIPITY

Sometimes defined as "a happy accident", serendipity is the discovery of valuable things that you weren't actually looking for. By definition, you can't *make* serendipity happen, but you can increase its likelihood by trying new things.

UNEXPECTED INVENTIONS

Many of the world's greatest inventions were the result of accidents or mistakes. A classic example was the invention of mauve, a purple dye. It emerged, quite by chance, from the search for a cure for malaria.

For centuries, it had been known that quinine was an effective way to treat malaria. Unfortunately, natural supplies were limited, and by the 19th century chemists were keen to find a way to make quinine artificially. One such chemist was William Perkin. In one attempt, Perkin created a dark substance that dissolved in alcohol to form a purple liquid. He discovered that the liquid was an effective dye for fabric. Perkin had accidentally invented the first synthetic dye.

HELPING ACCIDENTS TO HAPPEN

One way to encourage serendipity is to set yourself an arbitrary task that takes you out of your normal experience. As an example, the British comedian Dave Gorman took on a bet to find 54 people across the world who shared his name. The task itself was pointless, but it captured the public's imagination. He has now turned his experiences into a TV programme, an off-Broadway show and a book.

ENCOURAGING
SERENDIPITY

What pointless challenge can you set yourself to make serendipity possible? You could try the following examples.

*   *   *   *   *

Take a different route to work, or use another form of transportation.

Buy a magazine that you've never looked at before and read the editorial.

Choose a different time of year to go on vacation.

Buy an item from a store that you've never entered before.

Look in your local newspaper or library at the list of public events going on next week. Pick the third one and go to it.

Go to a section of a bookstore that you don't normally visit and choose a book with a title that catches your interest. Any book, from a novel to a "how to" book, might take you on a fascinating journey in your mind.

Next time you go out for a meal, choose a restaurant at random.

Become famous for five minutes. Phone up a local radio show to talk about a topic that interests you — or just enter one of their competitions.

Buy the current number 10 record in the pop charts. (Don't pick number one, as there's a chance you've heard it already.) Learn the lyrics, find out about the artists, then get somebody to test you on the lyrics.

WHEN WORDS COLLIDE

One way to spark your imagination is by adding a completely unrelated word to your current thinking. The random word gives your mind something new to focus on. In addition, using a random word allows you to come up with "silly" or "off-the-wall" ideas, and takes some of the pressure off, so you don't feel you have to come up with a "correct" answer.

PICK A WORD, ANY WORD

You can find a random word simply by opening a dictionary and choosing the first noun that you find. For example, if you're trying to think of uses for a dried-up ballpoint pen (remember the example on page 16), you might randomly pick the word "hairstyle" from the dictionary. How can you link "hairstyle" to using a dried-up pen?

Perhaps you could do it in the following ways:

- Use the pen as a hair curler.
- Cut the pen up into small hoops and use them as hair beads.
- Use the shaft of the pen to store strands of hair (or other long, thin things).
- Use it as a comb.

These ideas weren't in the original list of possible uses, and you can probably think of more. Indeed, some people actually find more ideas when they're given a random word to work with than they do when they have a free choice! (See also "Picking a theme", page 101.)

COMBINING WORDS AND IDEAS

With practice, the random-word technique can be used in just about any situation, from inventing a new product to re-thinking the best way to collect taxes. On the following page you'll find a small selection of words to get you started. Follow this simple step-by-step process to combine these words with your plans and see what results:

1   **Be clear about what you're looking for.**
    For example, you could state your challenge like this: "Come up with ideas for a venue where we can hold a 40th birthday party."

2   **Pick a number at random between 1 and 60.**
    To make it truly random, look at your watch or clock and check the number of seconds past the minute at the instant you look. If it's 16 seconds past the minute, go with the number 16.

3   **Look at the list on the following page.**
    Find the number you've chosen, and look at the word beside it. However inappropriate the word might seem, this is the one that you'll be combining with your idea.

4   **List things that you associate with the item.**
    For example, if you choose 16, "Umbrella", you might think of: wet weather, umbrella stands, paintings in which umbrellas appear, umbrellas as walking sticks, Gene Kelly in *Singin' in the Rain*.

5   **Incorporate that word into your problem.**
    For example, re-define the challenge as: "Come up with ideas for a 40th birthday venue linked to 'umbrellas'."

6   **Let the ideas flow.**
    For example, "Go somewhere that requires an umbrella, such as

a tropical rainforest … or a place nearer to home that has an artificial rainforest (botanical gardens). Or what about an old hotel where they still have umbrella stands?"

LIST OF RANDOM WORDS

1	Rabbit	21	Concrete	41	Gravestone
2	Tooth	22	Snowball	42	Robin
3	Yoga	23	Fireplace	43	Smoke
4	Suitcase	24	Nail polish	44	Trombone
5	Budgerigar	25	Calculator	45	Cat food
6	Crystals	26	Syringe	46	Ladder
7	Nail-clippers	27	Broccoli	47	Opera
8	Basketball	28	Swing	48	Fencing
9	Feathers	29	Seatbelt	49	Drainpipes
10	Goat	30	Top hat	50	Cave
11	Nun	31	Toenails	51	Seagull
12	Cliffs	32	Gold	52	Oxygen
13	Hammer	33	Cherry tree	53	Astronaut
14	Camera	34	Chocolate	54	Vikings
15	Bacon	35	Quiz show	55	Rodeo
16	Umbrella	36	Violin	56	Whispers
17	Bow tie	37	Shampoo	57	X-ray
18	Maple leaf	38	Iceberg	58	Apple
19	Barbed wire	39	Kennel	59	Helicopter
20	Taxicab	40	Pajamas	60	Purse

PICKING A THEME

As you might have seen from the "random words" exercise on page 98, the more freedom you have to express your ideas, the harder it can be to find inspiration. Your thinking can be more productive if you have a theme to give you a framework for your thoughts.

CONCENTRATING YOUR MIND

If a project is too open-ended, you can be dazzled by the endless choice, and if you aren't careful you can find yourself flitting from one idea to the next, without anything to direct you. Far from constraining you, a theme can focus your thinking. That's why the outfits that people wear at a themed costume or fancy dress party ("Heroes and Villains", say) are usually more imaginative than those at parties for which the invitations simply say "wear a costume".

There are no rules about how to choose a good theme – you'll just know one when you see it. Once you've chosen the theme, you should stick with it for long enough so that you can explore all the possibilities associated with it.

Some possible themes that you could try include a colour or shape, or a specific event in your life (such as your child's first day at school). Alternatively, you could seek inspiration from a famous person's life or actions (see also page 84). Sometimes, a theme might be suggested by an aspect of the project you're working on (as shown in the examples on the following page) – if so, run with it.

FAMOUS THEMED CREATIONS

Themes are an extremely powerful way of portraying "the big idea" behind a project and can inspire all sorts of spin-off ideas. Here are some examples showing how particular themes have been used in music, architecture and literature.

- **Creating music for movies**

  Composers of movie music often draw inspiration from the title. Ron Goodwin, who wrote the music for several big war movies, was keen on this technique. For the movie *633 Squadron*, he used the title to inspire the main rhythm: a rapid six beats followed by a slow three beats (one-two-three-four-five-six-ONE-TWO-THREE).

- **Creating a building**

  The Capitol Tower in Hollywood, built in 1956, was the world's first circular office building. Capitol Records' business was selling records, so the inspiration for the look of the building was a simple, if radical one: to build a tower that looked like a stack of records on a turntable. Today, office buildings with a circular cross-section have become commonplace throughout the world.

- **Creating a story**

  There are countless books in which a story is built from a simple theme. It might be a location, such as the beach in Thailand that inspired *The Beach*, or an object, such as the Vermeer painting that inspired *Girl with a Pearl Earring*. An extreme example is *La Disparition*, a French novel by Georges Perec, in which he imposed on himself the constraint of never using the letter "e". This must have forced him to explore language and expression to the limits.

HAVING A PLAN B

When you're caught up in an idea, you might not think to look for other avenues to explore. Having one big idea is exciting, but a few hours or minutes considering a "Plan B" will be time well spent. The mathematician James Yorke, expert on chaos theory, puts it in a nutshell: "The most successful people are those who are good at Plan B."

ADDITIONAL INSPIRATION

Coming up with a Plan B is never easy. When you're getting stuck into an idea, and being carried along by the momentum, it's really difficult to let go. This is fine if you find the idea works, but, more often, when you reflect on a concept, you begin to see its flaws and it doesn't seem so great after all. The Plan B approach not only gives you a fall-back option, it can often improve the quality of your main idea.

A USEFUL CATALYST
A team was asked to come up with ideas for promoting a new science exhibition at a museum. They became hooked on a concept that would involve staff dressing up as atoms and walking around the city linked together as a "molecule". It was suggested that they spend a few moments on a Plan B. There was some resistance, because they were enjoying themselves with the first idea. However, within 10 minutes, they had produced an idea for advertising on trains, which they started to prefer to the first notion. In the end, they combined the two: the carriages became the atoms that were linked to make the molecule.

CHAPTER 5

BEING CREATIVE WITH OTHERS

Holding discussions 106

Swapping ideas 108

Working in large groups 112

Brainstorming 114

When differences get personal 116

Suggest, don't propose 119

Finding three positives 121

Looking for a third way 124

Seeing the funny side 126

Creative thinking doesn't have to be a lonely experience. One of the most effective ways to generate ideas is to share your thoughts with someone else. Couples or teams can create an energy from which ideas take flight.

But being creative with others is also fraught with problems. We all spend so much of our lives talking to people that we assume we know how to work together naturally. Sadly, this is far from true. When opinions differ and emotions run hot, it's much harder to think out of the box without causing offence or a hostile reaction. In these circumstances, you need to develop a diplomatic approach to introducing new ideas. This chapter looks at some of the common problems that arise when pairs and larger groups try to generate ideas, and offers some practical ways to overcome them.

HOLDING DISCUSSIONS

Swapping ideas with others can be fun, if you do it the right way. It's most likely to work if everyone feels comfortable about offering their thoughts. This doesn't happen as a matter of course – you need to work on creating an atmosphere in which everyone feels secure and respected.

BARRIERS TO WATCH OUT FOR

You'd think a creative discussion should be a simple process: one person has an idea, then somebody else chips in, and this exchange goes on until a brilliant concept leaps out, at which point everything stops. However, that isn't how things usually happen in real life.

The truth is that all sorts of issues can hinder a free exchange of ideas. The following factors are the biggest barriers.

- **Anxiety**
  You never quite know how your idea will be taken until you've voiced it. The questions "Will they laugh at me?" or "Will this idea upset them?" can be enough to prevent you from putting it forward, especially if you lack confidence. Better to say nothing than to open your mouth and make a fool of yourself.

- **Status**
  In many situations, the people involved have different status: you and your boss, or you and your assistant, or an expert and a beginner. Both parties might be reticent about offering ideas. The lower-status person might feel their ideas are naïve, even

disrespectful. The one with higher status won't want to offer a "silly" idea because it might undermine their authority.

- **Opposing views**

    If your views don't overlap with those of the people around you, then you'll find it almost impossible to let ideas flow. Every time you hear an idea, you'll find yourself wanting to reject it. Similarly, your ideas might be squashed. When was the last time you saw a Republican politician happily trading ideas with a Democrat, or a Creationist with an Evolutionist? It just doesn't happen!

- **Thinking speed**

    People think at different speeds. In discussions, one person may find that by the time his or her idea has formed, the conversation has moved on — so that person keeps quiet. Do ideas come to you quickly, or do you need time to think?

IMPROVING YOUR INTERACTIONS

If you want to collaborate creatively with other people, you can improve your interactions in several ways.

DO set an initial period of criticism-free thinking (see page 114), so that everyone knows it will be safe to put forward ideas without them being ridiculed.

DO choose good listeners, whose opinions you respect.

DO allow some periods of personal thinking time, so that everyone can keep up with the flow of ideas.

DON'T choose people whose views are polar opposites to yours (or if you do, don't expect them to be receptive to any of your ideas).

SWAPPING IDEAS

When you're having creative discussions with other people, you'll find yourself dividing your time between two roles. Part of the time you'll be giving ideas to others; the rest of the time you'll be receiving their thoughts. You need to be able to work within each role effectively to have the best chance of generating ideas.

IDEA-GIVING AND IDEA-SELLING

Why might you give an idea to somebody else? You could be sounding them out to see what they think of your idea. Or you might be working jointly with them to come up with creative ideas, and this is your contribution. Or perhaps you want to persuade them to take your idea on board, but find that they need to be convinced. Each of these situations counts as "idea-giving", but you'll need different tactics to ensure a creative outcome.

If you're testing out an idea ...

Let your colleagues know what kind of response you're looking for. Sometimes, you might float ideas because you need support. If you've set your heart on resigning from your job to travel around the world, the last thing you'll want to hear is, "What, are you crazy? This'll be a disaster for your career!" So before you pass on the idea, define what you need by saying something like: "I need some reassurance – give me some reasons why I'm doing the right thing!"

On the other hand, you might be testing out an idea and looking for constructive criticism. If you know your idea is half-baked, warn your listeners that it needs to be built on, and ask them to suggest ways in which you can improve it.

If you and others are jointly producing ideas ...

Set some ground rules at the start, to make sure ideas flow freely and people stick to the point of the discussion. The simplest rule is that you'll have an initial period when you all put forward ideas without any evaluation. If this rule isn't set at the start, there's a danger that people will all too quickly criticize and squash each other's ideas.

Each person will naturally be more interested in their own ideas than anyone else's, but don't assume that your ideas will all be heard or recorded. If you have ideas that don't seem to have been taken up, make a note of them – you might be able to use them yourself.

If you're "selling" ideas to others ...

You may be convinced of the merits of your idea, but why should the other person "buy"? Imagine how you'd go about selling something to a sceptical purchaser. First, you need to draw their attention to the problem that your idea is helping to solve. Then tell them the benefits of the idea, including the opportunities that it might open up. Finally, rather than presenting the idea as a finished article, let the other person adapt and build on it. People are generally much more receptive to ideas if they feel some ownership and if you let them participate in the creative process.

IDEA-RECEIVING

We'd probably all prefer to think of ourselves as idea-givers – after all, that sounds like the creative bit. Yet arguably the more important role is idea-receiving.

If you want somebody else to help you generate ideas, then your responses to your friends' or colleagues' thoughts will have a huge bearing on whether they give you plenty of material to work with, or dry up after only a couple of suggestions. Here are some tips for being a creative idea-receiver:

Say what you need

Explain the problem clearly, and tell the other person which aspect you need their help with – otherwise, how can you expect them to come up with suitable ideas? This point may sound obvious, yet all too often you'll hear somebody asking for ideas and being met with silence because the other person doesn't know how to respond. Briefing your listener clearly will enable you to make the most of their contribution.

Welcome all suggestions

Don't set the standard of ideas too high. If you do, you may not get any suggestions at all, because the idea-giver will censor themselves. You can help by offering some rules, such as, "Please give me any idea, no matter how dumb you think it is." To make the idea-giver more comfortable, you can deliberately suggest a weak or silly idea as an example. Your listener might then feel more confident that they can do better, and is more likely to offer a suggestion.

Always respond

Whenever you receive an idea, you should acknowledge it and preferably give some constructive feedback. Otherwise, the idea-giver will assume that they've failed or you're not interested. To me this is the golden rule of idea-receiving, yet it's broken depressingly often.

I saw an example of a successful suggestion scheme at the BBC's recording studios, in the days before e-mail. In each studio was a book where users could comment on the equipment and suggest any improvements. The book was brimming with comments. The reason was that there was a rule for giving feedback: every idea had to get a handwritten response within 24 hours, even if it was simply, "Thank you, this is a complicated issue. We're looking into it." People felt that their comments mattered, so they continued to make suggestions.

If you can't respond to every idea, at least let people know how much feedback you can handle. A company I once worked with had what they called the "Unsolicited Ideas Box". This box was there for every employee to use. It came with a promise that every idea put in the box would be read by the CEO, even if the person suggesting it remained anonymous. For people who wanted feedback, there was a more formal suggestion scheme. The Unsolicited Box proved to be at least as popular as the formal scheme.

"To profit from good advice requires more wisdom than to give it."

Wilson Mizner, playwright (1876–1933)

WORKING IN LARGE GROUPS

If you've ever been out with a big group of friends, trying to decide where to go for dinner, you'll know that discussions involving lots of people can be a nightmare. In situations like this, you need to split people into smaller groups and make sure everyone has a chance to speak if they want to.

THE DANGERS OF GROUP-THINK

The same problems tend to arise in any group situation, from a formal meeting at work to a family discussion. Everyone has an opinion, two or three people might be talking at once, some might not be listening, and most of them are hoping that someone else will make a decision. Usually the outcome is something safe but dull, and people grudgingly go along with it because they don't want to rock the boat.

In large groups, two or three people will tend to dominate almost all of the conversation. The rest stay silent because they're anxious about offering ideas to a large audience, or they don't get a chance to interject because other people talk over them.

MAKING IT SAFE TO OFFER IDEAS

Break the large group into smaller groups, or even pairs. Five pairs will have far more ideas in one minute than one group of 10 people. In addition, everyone finds it easier to suggest ideas to one person rather than 10, and the fact that there are other groups thinking about the same issues can bring out a little competitive edge to spur people on.

MANAGING GROUPS

If you're the person running a group discussion, try these tips to enable everyone to contribute. You should soon notice the room fill with an energetic buzz as the ideas flow.

* * * * *

Open the discussion with an ice-breaker, to make people relax. For example, you could ask each person an easy, open question, such as, "What was the most fun thing you did last week?" Or you could encourage people to engage with the topic of discussion by asking, "What would you most like to come out of this discussion?"

* * *

To get the ball rolling, start by suggesting a really bad idea and admit to the group that it's lousy! By doing so, you're giving the message that it's all right to offer any idea, however stupid it may seem. As a result, others will feel more confident about putting forward their suggestions.

* * *

Allow anonymity. Not everyone wants to be noticed or wishes to have their name linked to an idea, especially if it's a controversial one. Rather than making people say their ideas out loud, you could ask everyone to write them on slips of paper, and collect them in a bucket, or even give people Post-It® note pads and get them to stick their ideas on a wall.

* * *

If you're asking people to put their ideas to the group, don't allow a free-for-all — invite each individual or pair in turn to contribute. Never assume that because a person says nothing, they have nothing to say. However, if someone feels they have nothing to offer, that's fine as well.

BRAINSTORMING

The Nobel laureate Linus Pauling stated that "the best way to have a good idea is to have lots of ideas". One of the most powerful tools for generating ideas is brainstorming – a technique designed to maximize creative thinking.

THE ORIGINAL RULES

People use the word "brainstorming" for any meeting in which people generate ideas. However, true brainstorming follows four main rules that were created in the 1930s, by advertising executive Alex Osborn, for use in his own company:

- **No criticism**

  During the idea-generating period, all ideas must be recorded. No negative comments are allowed and no idea should be rejected.

- **Quantity, not quality**

  You should aim for 100 crazy ideas rather than 10 good ones. The thinking behind this is that, as Osborn said, "It's easier to tone down a wild idea than to think up a new one."

- **Freewheel**

  Once the process has begun, you should allow the discussion to go where it wants to go.

- **Build**

  A successful brainstorm is one in which people pick up others' ideas and build on them. If you hear an idea and you respond by saying "Yes and … ", then that means you're building.

STRUCTURING A SESSION

You can carry out brainstorming with any number of people – you can even do it on your own if you really want to. However, you need to structure the session, otherwise people will get muddled about what they're supposed to be doing. A common problem is that one person will jump in with an idea, another will dismiss it, then there'll be a heated debate, and finally someone else will pipe up with, "What are we actually trying to solve here?"

One simple structure, which you can use in any creative-thinking session, works on the P I E principle, as shown in the box below. This structure has three stages: by keeping the stages separate, you focus people's minds on particular tasks. That way, you ensure that everyone's energy is devoted to coming up with ideas, rather than worrying about what their role is.

P is for problem	Start by agreeing what it is you actually want ideas for, and set the rules for the meeting at the same time. Otherwise, you'll find everyone will come up with their own, different view of what they're supposed to be doing.
I is for ideas	Once you've agreed what you want ideas for, you should then have the "brainstorming" phase – all ideas welcome, no criticism allowed.
E is for evaluation	This is the stage when you're allowed to criticize ideas (constructively), and pick out the ones that have the most potential.

WHEN DIFFERENCES GET PERSONAL

Many conversations that are intended to be creative end up as little more than exchanges of abuse – instead of a hothouse of innovation, you have a madhouse of people shouting, and the ideas get lost in the noise. However, you can defuse the situation before it gets too bad.

THE WAR OF THE WORDS

How do arguments happen? Often, disputes flare up because the participants are so determined to push their own ideas that they don't allow any building to happen. Not only do they air their own opinions forcefully, but they're all too often sarcastic or dismissive of other people's ideas. What was meant to be an idea-generating discussion becomes an idea-killing argument. Even more than self-criticism, hostile or dismissive reactions from others can make people hesitant about giving ideas, and can snuff out their creative spark.

HOW IDEA-KILLING HAPPENS

The diagram opposite indicates how the vicious circle can begin. It can all happen so quickly, too. (This image may remind of you of the self-imposed vicious circle of anxiety, on page 31.)

Becky gives an idea to Andy, who sees only the negative aspects, so rejects it. Becky feels affronted by his response. To regain her status, Becky looks for faults in Andy's next idea. He, in turn, takes revenge, and the discussion descends into a conflict.

Andy rejects
Becky's idea

Andy feels
criticized

**IDEA-KILLING:
THE VICIOUS CIRCLE**

Becky feels
defensive

Becky takes
revenge by
rejecting Andy's
next idea

This vicious circle arises so often in conversations that you shouldn't have much difficulty spotting it, at home or in the workplace. This is how many family arguments start.

GETTING THINGS BACK ON TRACK

Next time you find yourself involved in an idea-killing conversation, see if you can break the circle. You need to remember one of the basic rules of creative discussions – generating an atmosphere in which people feel confident and supported, not "got at" and defensive.

The easy way to do this is to accentuate the positive. As soon as someone offers their idea, pick out the good points and build on them, using language such as, "That's a good idea, and what you could do is …," or, "Yes, and that would help because …" (The words

"Yes, and … " at the start of a sentence are powerful as a way of encouraging creative thinking.)

What's remarkable is that you can, with practice, develop the knack of turning a vicious circle of idea-killing into a virtuous circle of idea-building. The secret is simply to react positively to somebody's idea. They, in turn, will be inclined to be positive about your ideas.

HOW IDEA-BUILDING HAPPENS

The diagram below shows how to generate a virtuous circle in which ideas flow freely. Note that the responses are positive from the outset. Becky gives an idea to Andy, who might not totally like it, but still looks for positive points. He builds on those points by saying "Yes, and … " Becky feels encouraged by his reaction, and more receptive to his ideas. She responds positively to Andy's next idea. Both are now in the right frame of mind to come up with new ideas and solutions.

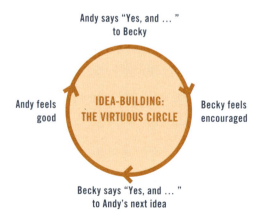

Andy says "Yes, and … " to Becky

Andy feels good

IDEA-BUILDING: THE VIRTUOUS CIRCLE

Becky feels encouraged

Becky says "Yes, and … " to Andy's next idea

SUGGEST, DON'T PROPOSE

If there are any tensions in a discussion, the way you present ideas could make the difference between building bridges and hostile rejection. If you tell people what to do, you risk putting them on the defensive. However, if you offer ideas as suggestions, you leave other people space to add their views.

ENCOURAGING AGREEMENT

Psychologists have found that in general the more assertively you express an idea, the more likely it is that the person hearing it will resist it. In his book *Improve Your People Skills*, Peter Honey described an experiment in which people offered ideas in one of two ways:

- **Proposing** (when the idea is given as a statement, such as "What you should do is … ")
- **Suggesting** (when the idea is expressed as a question or a reflection: "I wonder if … ?")

The discussions were observed, to see how the idea-receivers reacted to the ideas that they were given.

The results were remarkable. When an idea was proposed, almost half of the recipients received it sceptically and expressed difficulties with it. Yet when the same idea was merely suggested, only one in five recipients stated difficulties. The more moderate way of putting forward an idea almost doubled the chance of the recipient supporting it, and halved the number of negatives.

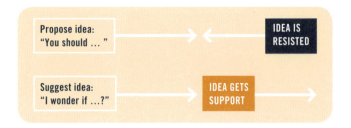

| Propose idea: "You should … " | → ← | IDEA IS RESISTED |
| Suggest idea: "I wonder if …?" | → | IDEA GETS SUPPORT → |

CHOOSING THE RIGHT WORDS

As the diagram above shows, if you suggest ideas they're more likely to be taken up and developed than if you propose them. Listen to yourself and others discussing ideas and observe how people respond depending on the style in which the ideas are presented.

If you're dealing with somebody whom you expect to be defensive when you offer ideas, think twice before starting with words like these:

- "What you should do is … "
- "I think you ought to … "
- "The best idea would be to … "
- "If I were you I would … "

Instead, put forward your idea in "suggestion" form. Where possible, take out references to "you", and make the suggestion impersonal, as in the following examples:

- "I wonder if it would be possible to … "
- "Has anyone ever thought of … "
- "I don't suppose we could … "
- "What if it were … "

FINDING THREE POSITIVES

I mentioned on page 35 that most people tend to see what's wrong with someone else's idea before they see the good points. If there are already tensions in the air, this critical attitude is only going to make them worse. To take the heat out of things, simply look for three positive points in the idea, and go from there.

GIVE THE POSITIVES FIRST

Rejecting a new idea is a normal reaction – even more so when the idea is about an issue close to your heart. Unfortunately, by doing so, you send out signals that you're not receptive to change. Not only do you close off that avenue for exploration, but you also tread on the other person's ego.

Nobody enjoys having their ideas squashed, so this person is likely to react defensively, especially if they also feel strongly about the issue. You risk getting into the sort of "idea-killing" argument described on page 116. To stop this happening, you need to take a deep breath and look on the positive side.

If someone offers an idea to which you feel hostile, build on it by deliberately looking for three good things that you can say about it, before you allow yourself to say anything negative. If your positive comments outweigh the negatives, the other person will feel reassured that you're considering their idea fairly and is likely to be more receptive to what you say.

PUTTING IT INTO PRACTICE

You'll probably find it's relatively easy to think of one positive thing, but often difficult to think of the second and third. A conversation in which three positives are given might go something like this:

Person A:
"What you should do is … "

Person B:
(secretly biting tongue)
"What I like about that suggestion is:
  it would …
  and it would …
  and another advantage would be …
However, how could we do it without . . . "

This does put all the pressure on Person B. It takes broad shoulders to be constructive about an idea in this way, especially if the idea is an implied criticism of what you've already done. But by giving three positives first, Person B can then be constructively critical without offending Person A. This approach might also generate an alternative idea that both of you like.

Wedding plans

Here's an example of how an exchange might go. Weddings are notoriously delicate areas for idea-giving.

Daughter:
"We're just starting to come up with ideas for the wedding."

Mother:
"I think you should hold it in the family church – it'll be the perfect place to bring all of your relations together."

Daughter:
(who has in mind a small humanist ritual somewhere out of town)
"Well, what I like about that idea is:

> *I think churches are a good way of making it a spiritual event.*
> *I do want to have close family members there.*
> *It's important that the venue has some meaning for us."*

Only now does she express her reservations:
"However, Peter and I don't want a traditional religious service, and we'd prefer to have the wedding in a place that has spiritual significance for both of us."

At this point, the family church idea might be rejected, but at least the daughter has now helped to clarify what she's looking for. By thinking through some of the benefits of her mother's idea, she might find some elements that she could take on board. In addition, the even-handed nature of the discussion might make her mother feel more positive about the eventual result, because her feelings have been taken into consideration.

LOOKING FOR A THIRD WAY

The essence of successful negotiation is reaching a solution that everyone can accept. If you manage to do this by finding a compromise, all well and good. However, sometimes the middle ground doesn't fill anyone with enthusiasm. In that case, you need a new idea that will be equally appealing to everyone involved.

REACHING AGREEMENT

When foreign leaders get together to exchange ideas about saving the planet or preventing war, diplomacy is essential to their discussions. If you listen to a joint press conference held by two countries that are known to have major differences in policy, what will stand out is the effort that both countries' leaders or spokespeople make to emphasize the areas where they agree.

Finding common ground between people is just as relevant on an individual level as it is in international politics. It's a necessary goal whether you're debating with an ex-spouse where your children will go on vacation or deciding on the ceremony for a wedding between a Muslim and a Christian.

One way to generate new ideas in these circumstances is to begin by defining and agreeing on your objectives. What is it that both of you are trying to achieve? What issues are the most important for each of you? Once you have this framework for your discussion, you can think of ideas that will meet those objectives.

NOT BLACK, NOT WHITE, BUT YELLOW

There is, of course, a risk that you'll come up with a bland compromise that doesn't really satisfy anyone. (Indeed, one cynical definition of "compromise" is "a stalling between two fools".) If you think of one person's idea as "black" and the other's as "white", you could imagine the compromise idea as "grey". However, it might be possible to find a creative solution that excites both parties – you could think of this new idea as "yellow".

Black-and-white thinking is a particular hazard when emotions are involved. So, for example, a divorced couple might find themselves in the sort of tangle outlined in the box below. You can reach the "yellow" state by using some of the lateral thinking techniques described in Chapter 3, to help you decide what the real problem is and then bypass any areas where you're stuck.

FATHER'S VIEW (BLACK)	"The children should spend all their weekends with me!"
MOTHER'S VIEW (WHITE)	"The children should spend all their weekends with me!"
COMPROMISE (GREY)	"Let's have the children to stay on alternate weekends."
REAL ISSUE	Both parents want to do the things they have in common with the children (football, ballet).
CREATIVE SOLUTION (YELLOW)	Listen to what the children want! Plan a timetable in advance of each school term, according to the events that they want to attend.

SEEING THE FUNNY SIDE

Humour is one of the most effective ways to put across a difficult idea. It lightens the mood and takes the pressure off people to defend their opinions or protect their feelings. And, as explained on page 19, laughter – the "HA HA!" response – is one of the main triggers for creative ideas.

MANY A TRUE WORD IS SPOKEN IN JEST

Some of the most heartfelt opinions can be expressed only as comedy. That was one of the roles of the court jester in medieval times: the low-status fool was able to utter truths that would never be tolerated in those of high rank. George Bernard Shaw also recognized this point. In his words, "If you want to tell people the truth, you'd better make them laugh, otherwise they'll kill you."

People who are too shy to give their ideas formally often find it easier to speak up in a light-hearted setting. You have to make sure, though, that people laugh with rather than at each other. If one person feels that the joke's on them, they might be put off saying anything.

There are several ways in which you could use humour to put across a message. Here are just a few methods:

Turning things upside down

The technique of reversing ideas (see page 65) can help you generate new inspiration. It can also enable a light-hearted (but sometimes hard-hitting) discussion about a sensitive topic.

Using silly ideas

As we've already seen on page 110, if you want to give people confidence in their ideas it can help if you put forward a really silly or feeble one first. Perhaps you could ask your listeners to top it with an even more crazy or funny suggestion – amid all the laughter, they might come up with something amazing.

THE OPPOSITES GAME

Playing the "Opposites" game works particularly well in the workplace. For example, it's common for junior staff to complain about the need for "better communications". Instead of asking, "How could we make communications better?", to which the response is likely to be dark looks and silence, you can make a game of it: "How could we make communications as bad as possible?" This invariably generates laughter, particularly among teams where communication really is bad, and yet it allows people to state real concerns in a safe way.

Playing a role

Role-play is another useful technique. It can be easier to put across an uncomfortable idea if it's not "you" saying it. I've often had greater success suggesting an idea to my three-year-old daughter if it comes from Bertie the hand puppet than if I say it myself. If I tell her that she should eat up her cabbage, she'll just resist. But if Bertie suggests it, she often complies, or at least argues a reasonable case for not doing as I say. You might want to think twice before using a hand puppet with an adult, but anything that can inject a smile into the conversation is likely to make the exchange of ideas that much easier.

CHAPTER 6

MAKING IT HAPPEN

Setting a deadline 130
Beating the mid-project blues 132
Planning for the worst case 134
Ten words for creativity 135

It's one thing to have ideas, but unless something happens, creative thinking remains just that – thoughts that might be stimulating, but don't change anything. Once you've generated your ideas and thought them through, you need to act on them.

Taking on a new project can be daunting. You might dread the pressure of deadlines. You might begin well but succumb to the "mid-project blues", when you lose your impetus. And what if it all goes wrong? This chapter shows you how to meet these fears head-on and overcome them. The chapter ends with 10 words that will make you more creative. By using these words, you can start your new life of creativity straight away.

SETTING A DEADLINE

There can be so many pressures on your time that without discipline you find your creative project drifting, and weeks become months, and then years. Nothing focuses the mind better than deadlines. If you see a deadline as a challenge instead of a problem, it could help you toward your goal.

MEETING THE CHALLENGE

You might think that pressure stifles creative thinking, and sometimes this is true – under too much stress, you can panic and the mind goes blank. But more often, a deadline helps to get the creative juices going – if you know you have to deliver, you've no choice but to let some of your raw ideas get through. Without the constraint, you'd have time to think of a hundred reasons why the idea wouldn't work. Try the following tips to help you fix a goal and stick to it:

Set your own deadline

If your project doesn't already have a deadline, set yourself one. If it's a big project, break it down into a series of milestones. When you get to each milestone, you can take a breather and reflect on how you're doing and how to tackle your next one.

Promise others you'll do it

If you want to be sure that you'll complete a task, few inducements beat making a commitment to other people first. If you've volunteered to design the set for your local drama group's next production, you've no choice but to deliver ideas by a fixed date. Apart from anything else, you might see posters everywhere, reminding you of your deadline. When it comes to your own goals, you don't have to go as far as putting notices in public places, but you should commit in such a way that backing out would, at the very least, make you lose face.

PUTTING MYSELF ON THE LINE

Once, when preparing to give a talk, I decided on a dramatic opening. I'd get a friend to pretend to be me on stage, while I'd act as a member of the audience who suddenly interrupted the talk. However, as the day approached I began to get cold feet. I began to think that a normal lecture would be OK – and much less risky. However, I'd already told several respected colleagues that I was going to do the stunt. The risk of losing face with them was the only spur that drove me on. After the event (which went down a storm) I was glad to have gone through with it.

Keep reminding yourself

Another way of pushing yourself to be creative is to put up a sign in a prominent place that you know you'll look at every day. On the sign you should set out in big letters:

> **WHAT YOU WANT TO ACHIEVE**
> **WHY YOU WANT TO ACHIEVE IT**

Whenever you feel you're falling back into a rut or running out of steam, the sign will remind you why your goal is so important to you.

BEATING THE MID-PROJECT BLUES

I once met an architect who'd designed some of the world's most famous sports stadia. He said he found the best parts of a project were the beginning and the end. In the middle, he'd run into the "mid-project blues". This is a common problem in creative tasks. How can you overcome it?

WHAT CAUSES THE BLUES?

At the beginning of a project, you're likely to feel that everything is possible. There's all the excitement of doing something new combined with the stimulation of generating ideas without any constraints. And at the end, there's the satisfaction of achievement. For my architect friend, the thrill came from unveiling the finished building, the glory

Level of enthusiasm

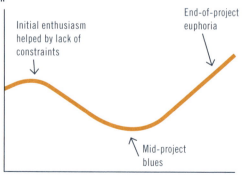

Initial enthusiasm helped by lack of constraints

End-of-project euphoria

Mid-project blues

Duration of project

of the press coverage and the pride in having overcome so many challenges. However, as the diagram opposite illustrates, it can be tough to sustain yourself through the day-to-day grind in the middle.

The excitements of beginning, and the euphoria at the end, can seem very far away when you're halfway through and facing a seemingly insurmountable problem. At these moments, it's common to find yourself thinking:

- "Why am I doing this?"
- "Are we going down a blind alley here?"
- "Are my ideas really that good?"
- "I'm just not making any progress."

OVERCOMING THE LOW POINTS

If your career depends on succeeding, that pressure is usually enough to push you through the low points. However, if you've nothing to spur you on except your pride, periods of self-doubt can feel threatening.

If you encounter the mid-project blues, refer to the following tips to urge yourself onward:

- Remember that everyone gets these feelings at some point.
- Take a break, to give yourself a chance to refresh your thinking.
- Remind yourself why you started this challenge in the first place – what was important to you, what you thought the difficulties would be and why it mattered so much to you.
- Re-energize yourself by coming up with more ideas. Another round of brainstorming (see page 114) can really help, even if it's on an unrelated subject, just to give you a dose of the feel-good factor.

PLANNING FOR THE WORST CASE

What if it all goes wrong? The prospect of failure is enough to stop you taking an idea further. And everyone has dark moments when all the weaknesses of an idea stare out at you and the merits disappear. Make plans now so you'll be able to cope if the unthinkable happens.

LOOK AT POTENTIAL PROBLEMS

What's the worst that could happen? You get laughed at? You lose money? If you set out all the things that might go wrong, you can begin to plan for them and think how to minimize their impact. If you can't face the prospect of giving up your job to take on a new, risky venture, is it possible to start the project in your spare time or when you're on leave? Or could you negotiate some "time out"? It would also help to have a Plan B, as described on page 103.

THINK OF THE BENEFITS

Think back about risks that you've already taken (learning to windsurf, or adopting a child). Looking back, are you glad that you took those risks or do you have any regrets? Are there risks that you didn't take but wish you had?

I had a friend whose mantra was: "I've never taken a risk that I regretted." Perhaps the same is true for you – some or all of the risks you've taken might have enriched your life. If that's true, use your past experience to strengthen your resolve to take the next risk.

TEN WORDS FOR CREATIVITY

Creative thinkers come in many forms, but they belong to
one of five types: the child-like thinker, the problem-solver,
the dreamer, the builder and the "imagineer". You can use
each type of outlook to spark your own creativity.

DIFFERENT APPROACHES

For each type of creative thinker, there are two words that sum up
the way they approach life. These words are given in the box below.

TYPE	CHARACTERISTICS	WORDS
Child-like	Has the curiosity and confidence to explore ideas.	"Why not?"
Problem-solver	Regards every setback or block as a problem to be solved.	"How to … "
Dreamer	Aspires to what might be, rather than what is.	"I wish … "
Builder	Supports other people's ideas and knows how to build on them.	"Yes, and … "
Imagineer	Is ready to think the unthinkable and explore the unknown.	"What if?"

You can benefit from all of these approaches. Simply use each pair of
words in everyday life, starting now. Almost without realizing it, you'll
start to adopt the attitudes of a creative thinker. It's as easy as that.

SOLUTIONS

PAGE 8: JOINING THE DOTS

This is the classic solution for the nine-dot puzzle.

PAGE 14: THE SWIMMING POOL PUZZLE

If you turn the square 45°, you can increase it to twice the size and still fit it between the trees.

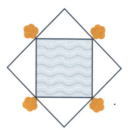

PAGE 16: 101 USES FOR A DRIED-UP PEN

Possible uses for the inkless pen include:

Blowpipe, storage case for pins, whisky measure, model of a pen, quill, thermometer holder, seed dibber, lever, back-scratcher, toothpick, puncture repair tool, keyboard cleaner, pipette, whistle, catapult, door wedge, prop for a stage play, comb, stirrer, ring holder, knob at the end of a light cord, slider to run along a string, screwdriver, mashing device, insulator, conductor's baton, fishing rod, drumstick, drinking straw, wedge to prop open a window, sweetcorn holder, fine paintbrush handle, hole puncher, spring (use the bendy ink cartridge), roller for fine pastry.

PAGE 68: BREAKING OUT AGAIN

Here are some more solutions to the nine-dot puzzle, taking you even further "out of the box".

Nine dots in three lines:

If the dots are large enough, or the lines long and thin enough, this zig-zag solution will work. (Did you assume that the lines always had to go through the middle of the dots?)

Nine dots in one line:

With a fat enough pen, all you need is one thick line.

Other solutions include taping the paper around a tin can and drawing a diagonal line, or folding the paper and jamming the pen through the middle. (Some people regard this solution as cheating; others think it is a legitimate challenging of assumptions.) This question is often faced by innovators. There's no right answer!

The 16-dot puzzle:

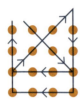

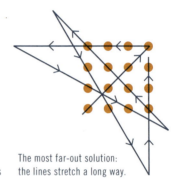

The "wisdom tooth" solution: this extension of the nine-dot solution goes out of the box in two directions.

The most far-out solution: the lines stretch a long way.

PAGE 69: PUZZLING QUESTIONS

1   Canadians (like everyone else) eat less in February for the simple reason that there are fewer days than in any other month.

2   Today is January 1, and Sally's birthday is December 31. Two days ago she was still 12, yesterday was her 13th birthday, at the end of this year she'll be 14, and at the end of next year she'll be 15.

3   E. The sequence consists of the initial letters of the number sequence "One", "Two", "Three", "Four" and so on.

INDEX

agreement 110, 124–5
"Aha!" moments 19, 46
aims *see* goals and
  objectives
answers 10, 15
anxiety 31, 106
arguments 116, 121
associations 80–1
assumptions,
  challenging 9, 66
attention levels 60
attitudes, of creative
  thinkers 20–1, 49

backtracking 28
barriers, to creative
  thinking 29–30
Beatles 92
blaming others 36–7
blocks (to creative
  thinking) 29–30,
  47, 83
blues, mid-project 132–3
Blumenthal, Heston 93
boredom 26
brainstorming 11, 47,
  114–15, 133
Buffy the Vampire Slayer
  64

camera obscura 46
Canaletto 46
challenges 44–6, 36–7,
  130

checklists: tips for
  getting started 48
children, creativity of 10,
  14–15, 39
child's eye view 54
collaboration 106–13
comfort zones 27–8
commitment 43, 131
comparing and
  contrasting situations
  62–3
competitions 49
compromise 124–5
concentration 60, 101
confidence 42, 44–6,
  29–30, 31
connections test 63
conversations 116–18
creative thinkers 20–1,
  135
creative thinking 10–11,
  135
  barriers to 29–30
  and daydreaming 60
  and humour 19,
    78, 91
  and imagination 20–1
  and lateral thinking
    51
  PIE principle 115
creative writing 11,
  44–5, 49
creativity 16, 21, 22, 62
  "Aha!" moment 19

  in children 10, 14–15,
    39, 54
  criteria for 23
  in day-to-day life
    20, 23
  developing prototypes
    70–1
  learning to be creative
    10–11
  and past experiences
    15
  ten words for 135
  using "tricks" 46
creativity myth 10
crises 28, 76

daydreaming 60
de Bono, Edward 51
de Mestrel, George
  77
de Staël, Madame 62
deadlines 30, 130–1
decisions, snap 28
demands, other people's
  43
diagrams 55, 80–1
difficulties 36–7
diplomacy 124
disagreements 107,
  116–18
discoveries, scientific
  71–2,
discussions 106–13,
  119–20, 121

dissatisfaction, as
    trigger for ideas 76–7
distractions 43, 82, 91
"Don't cry for me,
    Argentina" (Rice and
    Lloyd-Webber) 72–3
Dorothy (*Wizard of Oz*) 85
dreams, realizing 59

"Easy as ABC" puzzle 15
Edison, Thomas 19, 82
emotions 125
energy, mental 42, 78
enthusiasm 20, 42, 132
evaluation of ideas,
    premature 35
Evita (Rice and Lloyd-
    Webber) 72–3
exaggeration 89
excuses 29–30, 37
exercises *see* puzzles,
    games and exercises
expectations, misleading
    18
experiments
    Fuller, Buckminster 30
    Leonardo da Vinci 22
experts, and new ideas 38

failure, fear of 30, 134
fall-back options 103
Fat Duck restaurant 93
fear, of failure 30, 44
feedback 31–4, 111
figurative language 90–1
financial planning 34

Fleming, Alexander 71
flexibility 21
frustration 19, 26, 90
Fry, Art 73
Fuller, Buckminster 30

games *see* puzzles,
    games and exercises
getting started 47–9
goals and objectives 22,
    28, 43, 44, 82, 124
    "I wish" technique 61
    reinforcing 131
    working backwards
        from 59
Gorman, Dave 96
greetings cards, sending
    66
groups, working in 112
grumbling 36–7

Holmes, Sherlock 85
Honey, Peter, *Improve
    Your People Skills* 119
houses, moving 28, 67
"How to" technique 53
humour 19, 78, 91,
    126–7
"101 uses for a dried-up
    pen" game 16

"I wish" technique 61
ideas 20–1, 58, 60, 80
    alternative 103, 122
    children's 54
    combining 92–4

and creative blocks
    29
discussing 106–13,
    120
drafting 47
exchanging 108–11
killing 38, 116–18,
    121
original 92–3
recording 95
responses to 35, 111
sharing 16, 83,
    126–7
silly 110, 127
structuring 80–1
swapping 108–11
triggers for 28, 76–7
and words, combining
    99–100
illustrations, as aids to
    problem-solving 55
imagination 20–21, 40,
    59, 88
*Improve Your People
    Skills* (Honey) 119
information 60, 80
innovations 70–1
inspiration, moments
    of 19
inspirational people
    84–5
interactions, improving
    107
intuition 60
inventions, and
    serendipity 96

jargon 54
jobs, changing 26–7, 28, 34

knowledge, demonstrating 38–9
Koestler, Arthur 19, 77
Köhler, Wolfgang 82

lateral thinking 51
  exercises 68–9
  generating ideas 58
  re-framing problems 52–3
  "Why? Why?" technique 56–7
laughter, and creative thinking 78
Lennon, John 85
Leonardo da Vinci 22, 23, 46
lifestyle 10–11, 28
listeners, finding 83
low points, overcoming 133
Lubitsch, Ernst 84
lyric-writing 72–3

McCartney, Paul 72
mental energy 42, 78
mid-project blues 132–3
mind games, suggestions for 79
mistakes 30, 31
momentum, maintaining 28

motivation 37, 43, 91
moving house 28, 67
"Mozart effect" 78
Mozart, W. A. 23
multiple-choice questions 17
multi-way reversing 67
music, composing 82

names, memorable 17
negative feedback 31–4
nine-dot puzzle 8–9, 68
nitrous oxide (anaesthetic), discovery of 71–2
notes and sketches 95

Oasis 92
objectives see goals and objectives
opinions, other people's 29–30
"Opposites" game 127
originality 92–3
Osborn, Alex 114

Pauling, Linus 114
penicillin, discovery of 71
perfectionism 21
Perkin, William 96
personal blocks, identifying 29–30
personalities, of creative thinkers 20–1
perspectives, alternative 64

physical surroundings 29–30
Picasso 23
PIE principle 115
places, inspiring 42
"Plan B" approach 103
planning 34, 134
positive feedback 31–4
positives, identifying 121–3
Post-it® notes, invention of 73
"premature evaluation" 35
pressure 130
priorities, recognizing 59
problem-solving
  connections test 63
  famous problem-solvers 85
  "How to" technique 53
  "I wish" technique 61
  and irrational "play" 9
  multi-way reversing technique 67
  "Opposites" game 127
  PIE principle 115
  "Plan B" approach 103
  random words technique 98–100
  reversal technique 65–7, 126

the "three Ps" 23
"What if?" games
86–7
"Why? Why?"
technique 56–7
see also puzzles,
games and exercises
problems 53, 58, 82
explaining 55, 110
potential 134
and previous
experience 15, 18
prioritizing 59
re-framing 36–7
reversing 65–7
see also problem-
solving
product names, choosing
17
puzzles, games and
exercises 17
"101 uses for a dried-
up pen" 16
"Aha!" moment 19
connections test 63
"Easy as ABC" puzzle
15
for getting tasks
done 91
lateral thinking
exercises 68–9
making it simple 55
mind games,
suggestions for 79
multiple choice
questions 17

nine-dot puzzle 8–9,
68
"Opposites" game
127
puzzling questions 69
random words
exercises 98–100
16-dot puzzle 68–9
solutions to 136–8
swimming pool puzzle
14–15
"What if?" games
40–1, 86–7
see also problem-
solving

questions 17, 56–8,
69, 83
quiz shows, television
17, 94

random words technique
98–100
reality TV 64
responsibility, taking 37
reversal technique 65–7,
126
Rice, Tim 72
risk-taking 28, 49, 134
role models 84
role-playing 84–5, 127
routines 26
ruts 26–8, 34

second opinions, seeking
83

second thoughts 28
security 27
self-confidence 29–30
semantic maps 80–1
sensitive topics 126
serendipity, and
inventions 96–7
Shaw, George Bernard
126
Sherwood, Dennis 35
silly ideas 110, 127
Silver, Spencer 73
similes 90–1
Simpson, Homer 90
16-dot puzzle 68–9
solutions, imagining 55
solutions to puzzles
136–8
spider diagrams 80–1
status 106–7
stress 130
suggestions 110,
119–20
surroundings, physical
29–30
swimming pool puzzle
14–15
Sydney Opera House
70–1

"take a chance" attitude
49
television series
ideas for 94
quiz shows 17, 94
reality TV 64

tensions, in discussions 119–20, 121
Tharp, Twyla 92
The Art of Thought (Wallas) 83
"The Big Stink" 77
themes 101–2
thinkers, creative 20–1, 135
thinking, creative *see* creative thinking
third way, finding 124–5
thoughts 80–1
   communicating 90
   speed of 107
   see also creative thinking
three Ps criteria for creativity 23
time 10–11, 29–30, 43
"tricks" for creativity 46
triggers, for ideas 76–7
TV *see* television series

Utzen, Jørn 70

V22-Osprey 94
Velcro®, invention of 77
Vermeer 46
vicious circles 31, 34, 116–18
viewpoints, alternative 14, 19
virtuous circles 118

Wallas, Graham, *The Art of Thought* 83
warm-up, for mental energy 78
weaknesses, identifying 21
wedding plans 122–3
weight loss 34
Westwood, Vivienne 93
"What if?" games 86–7
Who Wants to be a Millionaire 94
Wife Swap 64
Wilder, Billy 84
willpower 34
words: random word technique 98–100
Wordsworth, William 90
worst case scenarios, planning for 134
"writer's block" 47
writing, creative 11, 44–5, 49

"Yesterday" (Lennon & McCartney) 72
Yorke, James 103

FURTHER READING

Edwards, Betty *Drawing on the Right Side of the Brain*, Simon & Schuster 1987

Feynman, Richard *What do you care what anyone else thinks?* Bantam 1988

Koestler, Arthur *The Act of Creation*, Penguin Arkana 1989

Nolan, Vincent *The Innovator's Handbook*, Sphere 1987

Roberts, R.M. *Serendipity, Accidental Discoveries in Science*, Wiley 1989

Sherwood, Dennis *Unlock Your Mind*, Gower 1998

Tharp, Twyla *The Creative Habit*, Simon & Schuster 2003

ROB EASTAWAY'S WEBSITE

If you'd like to find out more about Rob Eastaway and explore his ideas in greater depth, please visit his website, at www.robeastaway.com

AUTHOR'S ACKNOWLEDGMENTS

Writing a book on creative thinking can have its own ironies. What if you get stuck for ideas? ("Why not just read the first chapter of what you've written?" suggested one friend, helpfully.) I am particularly grateful to Phil Lowe for his many insights, and to Richard Harris and Martin Daniels, whose styles of creative feedback perfectly complement each other. Thanks also to Colin Mayes, Ed Smith, Michael Haslam, Joanna Griffiths, Chris Healey, Rachel O'Riordan and everyone else off whom I bounced ideas.

I've learned a great deal over the years by reading and talking about creativity. Two books, *The Innovator's Handbook* by Vincent Nolan and *The Act of Creation* by Arthur Koestler, have had particular influence in forming my ideas. I'm also indebted to my long-standing mentor Dennis Sherwood, who has given me several ideas for this book.

Creative thinking is so much easier when there are enthusiastic and supportive people to work with. Thanks to Charlotte Howard for setting this project in motion, to Caroline Ball and Katie John for being so involved and creative as editors, and to Elaine not only for all your constructive suggestions, but also for letting me spend so much time in the office while you were dealing with Jenna and Adam, who are already showing signs of creative thinking – and all the challenges that brings.